HOLIDAYS AND THE FEASTS

CHRISTMAS, EASTER, AND PAGANISM

NICHOLAS CAMPBELL

3rd Edition
REVISED & EXPANDED

3rd Edition, Copyright © 2023 Nicholas Campbell
Published by Christ is the Cure
Boerne, Texas
Cover Design by Rebekah Campbell

2nd Edition, 2021
1st Edition, 2020

ISBN: 979-8-9885721-2-1 [Paperback]
ISBN: 979-8-9885721-3-8 [Hardcover]

To my dear wife, who dedicated hours of support and labor in the production of this and past editions.

CONTENTS

PREFACE TO THE 2ND EDITION

Thank you for purchasing the second edition of this book. I hope it proves to be helpful in your study of the topics presented. When "Holidays and the Feasts" was first published in 2020, it was done quickly due to many pressing requests for transcriptions of the episodes featured on the Christ is the Cure podcast. Therefore, the book was essentially the compiled and edited notes from episodes 148, 155, and 156. Because of this, the formatting and writing style were fairly informal and unedited compared to traditional published works.

In this edition, I have taken the time to expand each of the sections with better articulations of previous arguments or new points altogether. This means the book now goes beyond what was put forward in the podcast episodes that inspired it. Hopefully you will find this edition more accessible with fewer typos and errors as I and my wife have reviewed and edited each section together in order to better polish the book. Another improvement is to the footnotes in each section. In the first edition I wrote,

"One thing to note is that there aren't many footnotes, and the ones that are present are put into the document as end notes. The reason for this is simple; in a podcast format, footnotes aren't possible or practical. That said, most (if not all), of the references and sources used for this work can be found on the resources and further reading pages."

This edition provides some corrections to this dilemma, but if there is a citation where a *formal footnote* isn't present, you can find the source either quoted in the text itself or in the bibliography. You will also find the sources from every section compiled at the end of the book.

Additionally, some of the discussions and information found in Episode 149 of the Christ is the Cure podcast has been added to this edition of the book in the relevant sections of part 2. The most considerable update to the 2nd edition is the new section, "Part 3: A Biblical Case for Celebrating Christmas." I hope you find this to be a welcomed and helpful addition to the book as you navigate the topic.

PREFACE TO THE 3RD EDITION

The third edition of this volume is predominately concerned with the book's layout and cosmetics. These changes aid in readability, but it is also worth mentioning that some of these changes are reorganizations of the book.

For example, the chapters on Sol Invictus, Winter Solstice, Saturnalia, and Pseudo-gods from the previous edition have been combined into a single chapter, "Assertions and Answers," in part two. Another example is that the Worldview/Presuppositions and Detours discussions have been added to their respective part's introductions. Additionally, footnotes have been converted to endnotes and grouped at the end of the book.

However, along with being revamped for readability, some changes have been made to the contents. This edition features a few expansions in parts one and four. Part one now expands on the subject of Passover in chapter three, while part four expands on numerous aspects of the Easter discussion. In addition, previous readers who have picked up the third edition will notice that Chrysostom's details from his homily on the dating of Christmas have been added to chapter six in part two. Previously, Chrysostom's account was briefly mentioned,

> "John notes that the celebration of the feast for the birth of Christ is an ancient tradition, and he appeals to Roman tax records known of the West."

This edition takes a moment to expand on Chryostom's testimony and briefly on the Chronograph of 354.

Concerning part four of this edition, there have been significant expansions in every chapter aside from the introduction and chapter twenty. Furthermore, a new chapter ("Cheap Paganism") has been added.

Lastly, this edition has included a conclusion and two appendices as a supplement, as the previous editions ended abruptly with no concluding remarks. I hope you find this short book to be a resource worth revisiting as you press into the subjects at hand.

INTRODUCTION

An entire book dedicated to the subject of Feasts, Christmas, and Easter may seem quite strange. Who in their right mind would spend so much time defending a tradition of men like Christmas? In truth, I never desired to dive into these topics publicly until a couple of years ago when I was working through them myself. It may surprise the reader to find that I struggled for years with celebrating Christmas, and grappled on occasion with whether or not I needed to observe the feasts of the Old Testament. For quite some time, I reluctantly allowed Christmas to be an event in my home. It was pagan in my mind, and had everything to do with excess and material-ism. On more than one occasion, I was ready to toss the tree, melt some ornaments, and never speak of the day again.[1] This perception felt sensical, given my upbringing in a non-religious home with a heavy secular and cultural observance of Christmas. Additionally, many Christians I knew had called the celebration pagan, including some church historians I respect dearly.

This attitude toward Christmas changed when I started noticing observances that were less focused on the secular, cultural, or materialistic elements, and more focused on Christ. I also began to see a disconnect in some Protestant circles over the holiday versus how other traditions in Christendom viewed Christmas. For example, Eastern Orthodox and Roman Catholics were adamantly opposed to the notion of Christmas being pagan.[2] Some of their points were compelling enough to spur me to view the subject with a more critical eye. I began to see how frequently arguments against Christmas were comprised of mixed and matched events, with an amplified and stacked rhetoric to seemingly add weight. Many also negated the concept of intent in the formation of the holiday, regardless of historical circumstances. Lastly, I noticed that the events of the Reformation and zeal against Roman Catholicism led to many exaggerated conceptions and arguments against the holidays, especially Christmas. A problem with these arguments is that the Eastern Orthodox, who were fairly disconnected from the Reformation, did not believe these holidays were pagan.

This led to completing my own research on Christmas and Paganism, which snowballed into the discussions on the Feasts and Easter. After publishing episode 148, I was critiqued with comments such as "Why are you spending so much time and effort trying to justify this tradition of men?" and "You're just tightly grasping to this holiday." This response was unexpected. I was bewildered by how many people opposed my defense of the early church's integrity. The reply that came to my mind was this: Why would you criticize, instead of rejoice, when someone spent the time to research these issues if they are important enough for you to critique? Aren't we both trying to call people to examine the issues and navigate them? Shouldn't we rejoice when individuals seek to defend the integrity of the early church?

The celebration of holidays and the feasts are worth discussing for a couple of reasons. First, finding what is appropriate for a Christian to celebrate is practical. I wanted to be able to put into practice what I believe, as I'm sure others who are navigating this topic wish to do as well. Pushback against the celebration of Christmas also drove this discussion, as I believe such strong opinions deserve a healthy response.

Secondly, the topic is worth discussing to defend the early church and its integrity. I struggle with the notion of it being painted as entirely corrupt and so desperate to look like the pagans of their day. This opinion is in direct opposition to much of what I have learned about the early church and how they went to great lengths to be dissimilar from the pagans. While I recognize that there are indeed errors and some assimilations in the early church, I do not believe such would be so drastic. How could the early church refuse instrumentation in worship because it was "too pagan," but be okay with adopting pagan holidays? How did such holidays then become so widely celebrated[3] in all of Christendom given their "pagan roots"?

The research and information compiled in this book has certainly been profitable in my personal studies, and I hope this volume likewise helps you navigate the subject of holidays and the feasts. Whether you end up agreeing with me or not, I pray it is beneficial and moves you to reflect on the glorious reality of the work of the triune God in redemption. I also ask that we can all move forward with unity in mind and Christ in heart on these issues, and recognize that the conclusions can be disagreed upon with love for the brethren still intact.

PART I
CHRISTIANS AND THE FEASTS

THE FEASTS

*I*n many evangelical circles, a notion is arising that Christians are obligated to keep the feasts given to Israel in the Old Testament. Such a notion often comes from a desire to be faithful and to find a more ancient and authentic faith held by Jesus and the apostles. Oftentimes, such notions are met with the idea that Christian holidays such as Christmas and Easter are unacceptable as they are not the God-ordained feasts of the Bible, but late (and often said; pagan) inventions. These individuals often say Christian holidays are traditions of men that undermine the commandments of God to observe his feasts.

In this part of the book, we will briefly discuss the feasts and answer the question of whether or not Christians are obligated to keep the feasts of the Old Testament. The search for a more historic and authentic faith is admirable, and we should encourage the heart behind that zeal on these issues. At the same time, we should also remember the freedom we have in Christ when it comes to this topic. Wherever one may fall on the issues presented, let us remember to love one another as disciples of Christ.

WHAT ARE THE FEASTS?

In general, the feasts are understood to be a celebration of seasons and special events. Due to societies' intrinsically connected life to religion in the pre-enlightenment era, these feasts often centered around a particular deity. When we get specific about feasts in regards to the Old Testament, the feasts can be defined as festivals given to Israel "as celebrations remembering God's great act of salvation in the history of his people."[1] The Old Testament feasts were often in cycles of seven as was the basis for much of Israel's worship. For example, the seventh day of the week was observed, along with the seventh month of the year, and these contained four of the feasts. In addition to these, the seventh year was observed along with the fiftieth year (the year of Jubilee), and this followed seven cycles, each made up of seven years. Finally, the feast of unleavened bread and the feast of tabernacles lasted for seven days.

The feasts mentioned within the Gospels include the feast of Unleavened Bread, Passover, Weeks, Tabernacles, and the feast of Dedication. Purim and New Moon were not mentioned, but are assumed. Passover is the most familiar because of its importance in the Gospels.

Passover has been argued to have begun among nomadic shepherds before the Exodus, and it involved the slaughter of a sheep or goat in the first month on the evening of the full moon (cf. Ex. 5:1-3; 12:21; 12:5; Deut. 16:2; 2 Chron. 35:7). It was the sprinkling of blood on the doorposts that brought identification for Israel and association with God's work in the Exodus (cf. Ex. 12:23; 23:15; 34:18). The association continued as time pressed on and the first month (Nisan on their calendar) became the month when future redemption was expected. The sacrifice of the Passover was to be roasted whole initially (Ex. 12:8-9; later it would be broiled), and it was to be eaten completely that night by the families who partook (Ex. 12:21: 43-49). Additionally, the people dressed to travel in order to reenact the Exodus so to speak (Ex. 12:11). Passover would later be added to the celebrations held specifically in Jerusalem, making it a pilgrim feast. This meant that an annual pilgrimage to Jerusalem would become normative for participating in the feast.

The feast of Unleavened Bread was held over seven days in the first month of Israel's calendar (which falls during March/April on our calendar). As the name of the festival suggests, it was a period of time when no leavened bread was to be eaten, sacrifices and grain offerings were to be made, and on the first and last days of the feasts, there was to be an assembling of the people (cf. Ex. 23:15; 34:18; Lev. 23:7-8; Num. 28:18-25). This was independent of Passover, but had the shared connection of the Exodus and both began in the same month. The two festivals were consecutive to one another, and eventually celebrated as one (cf. Ezra 6:19-22; Luke 22:1).[2]

The feast of Weeks (or the day of First Fruits or feast of Harvest; Ex. 23:14-17; 34:22-23; Num. 28:26) was to be celebrated fifty days after the raising of the sheaf of the first fruits at the end of Passover and Unleavened Bread (Lev. 23:9-16). This would eventually be known as Pentecost, a name that is first mentioned in intertestamental[3] writings. The feast was seen as being connected with the Exodus as well and by the 2nd century BC it was linked to the giving of the law and the covenants.

The Feast of Booths or Tabernacles is mentioned in all of the biblical calendars and was also called the feast of Ingathering, the feast of Yahweh, the feast to Yahweh, or just "The Feast." It was highly popular, important, and was a pilgrimage feast which followed the gathering of grain and the pressing of wine (Deut. 16:13). The greatest number of sacrifices were offered on this day (Num. 29:12-38). It was originally a seven-day feast (Deut. 16:15), and some believed it to be taken up from the Canaanites later on (cf. Judges 9:27; 21:19-21). The feast required people to live in booths (Lev. 23:42), temporary huts (Gen. 33:17), or tents (Josephus Ant. 3.244). The feast, like the others, was also connected to the Exodus. Jewish tradition, namely the Mishnah, notes a number of traditional celebrations surrounding the feast.

FEASTS NOT MENTIONED IN THE NEW TESTAMENT/ GOSPELS

The feast of Trumpets (Lev. 23:23-25) was the beginning of the civil new year. It consisted of a period of ten days of repentance beginning with Rosh Hashanah (the feast of Trumpets) as the first day, and Yom Kippur (the Day of Atonement) as the final day. Most of this festival was reliant on Jewish tradition, which held that God writes every person's words and deeds in the Book of Life, which he opens on this day to examine. If the good deeds outnumber the sinful ones, the person's name will be written in that book for another year on Yom Kippur. Yom Kippur, or the Day of Atonement, was the day instituted in Leviticus 23:26-32 when the high priest would sacrifice an animal to atone for the sins of the nation and intercede on their behalf. When the atonement was finished, a scapegoat was released into the wilderness to symbolically carry away Israel's sins. We will discuss Hanukkah in our discussion on Christmas,[4] but it is worth noting here that it is linked with the Maccabees in the intertestamental period. Purim is one of the most ambiguous holidays and is thought to celebrate the deliverance from Haman (cf. Esther 3:7). The New Moon feast was simply that - the start of each lunar month, marked with sacrifices and offerings.

JESUS AND THE FEASTS

*L*ooking at Jesus in relation to the feasts and what they signified will help us navigate this topic. Passover is the most emphasized feast in the Gospels. Jesus ate Passover with his disciples prior to his death. Following the meal, they sang a hymn as per custom and went to the Mount of Olives (Matthew 26:30). It is interesting that the hymn sung during Passover included a portion of Psalm 118:22, "The stone the builders rejected has become the Cornerstone," because we now know that it is Jesus who is called the Cornerstone that the builders rejected in Matthew 21:42 and 1 Peter 2:7. We find that Jesus is crucified as the Lamb of God, who is an atonement for sin (John 1:29). When Jesus institutes his supper as a covenantal meal during the Passover, he points to himself as being the Passover lamb. What the Passover signified in the past and pointed to in the future has come and is found in Christ (1 Cor. 5:7).

Unleavened bread (Matzah) was a symbol of Passover, and leaven is representative of sin (Luke 12:1; 1 Cor. 5:7-8). Matzah points to Jesus, the only one without sin. He is called the bread of God, the bread of life, and the bread that came down from heaven (John 6:32-48). Jesus as the sinless bread of life and the Passover lamb gives us a better understanding of Colossians 2:16-17: "Therefore, let no one pass judgment on you in question of food and drink, or with regard to a festival or a new moon or a Sabbath. These are a shadow of the things to come, but the substance belongs to Christ." We'll revisit Colossians 2 below.

The day of First Fruits was the day that Jesus rose on the third day of the Passover season (March or April, 16 Nissan) and is realized in Christ as "Christ has been raised from the dead, the first fruits of those who have fallen asleep" (1 Cor. 15:20). Paul in verse 23 also notes, "but each in his own order: Christ the first fruits, then at his coming those who belong to Christ." This celebration occurs in Christendom under the name of resurrection day or Easter - the "Christian" Passover or First Fruits.

Pentecost, or the feast of Weeks, is fascinating without doubt. Jesus told his disciples to wait in Jerusalem following his death, burial, resurrection, and ascension. When they were gathered for the feast of Weeks, on the 50th day after the Sabbath of Passover week, the Holy Spirit filled the house and filled the disciples (Acts 2). Peter points to this event as being a fulfillment of Joel 2:28-32. Pentecost, the feast of Harvest and God's blessing of harvest, is realized at the pouring out of the Spirit and the initiation of the New Covenant between God and Israel, which included the baptism of 3,000 individuals who are "harvested" in Acts 2:41.

The feast of Booths had two ceremonies in addition to residing in booths or tents. One involved the lighting of a giant lamp where individuals would carry torches and set them around the walls of the temple as a sign of the Messiah being a light to the Gentiles (Isaiah 49:6). Secondly, a priest would carry water from the pool of Siloam to the temple which pointed to when the Messiah would come and show the world that God covers the whole earth like the waters cover the sea. At the feast of Tabernacles, Jesus actually stated, "If anyone is thirsty let him come to me and drink" (John 7:37) and likely while the torches were burning, he said, "I am the light of the world" (John 8:12). Some also point to John 1:14, which says, "And the word became flesh and dwelt among us" implying that "dwelt" (σκηνοω) is the imagery of pitching a tent, and Jesus dwelling with the people. In either case, this is realized in Jesus' coming and his revelation.

FEASTS NOT MENTIONED IN THE NEW TESTAMENT

The Feast of Trumpets is often linked to the trumpets in Revelation, and is considered to be connected with the day of Judgment. The Book of Life is mentioned in Revelation 21:27, but the New Testament makes it clear that the only way to have your name in this book is through faith in Jesus. Those who are not found in the Book of Life, i.e. those who do not trust in the person and work of Jesus, will face judgment. When speaking about the Day of Atonement we note that Christ has become our new high priest, who entered into the true holy of holies (heaven itself) once and for all by his own blood (Hebrews 9:11-18). Some believe this festival finds its ultimate fulfillment when Jesus returns and Israel looks to him and repents (Zech. 12:10). Further, in this view it is believed that Israel will be forgiven and permanently restored (Rom. 11:26 and Isaiah 66:7-14).

JEWISH IDENTITY AND KEEPING THE FEASTS

*D*o Christians have to keep the feasts? At this point, we should have a general idea of how to answer this question. When looking through various articles written by Christian Jews and Gentiles, I found that most of them came to the conclusion that Christians are not required to keep the feasts. The feasts were given to Israel as national markers of identity.

If we look at the three texts of Romans 14, Galatians 3, and Colossians 2, we find that Gentiles are not bound to the feasts in the way that some insist. For example, Romans 14 points to the observance of feast days as being a matter of conscience. In this context, Paul is specifically speaking to the relationship between Jews and Gentiles in the Roman church. He knows the Jews keep the feasts and the Sabbath, yet he tells the community that the Gentiles are not bound to keep such customs or to observe the Sabbath(s). This conclusion of Paul would also apply to Jews who no longer observe their tradition.

Colossians indicates that the feasts were a shadow of the realities (or "substance") of Christ himself. A number of false teachers in Colossae were trying to disqualify the believers in regards to their practices (Col. 2:18). Paul notes that Christians are not under the Mosaic covenant, and are therefore no longer obligated to observe the Old Testament markers of Jewish ethnicity. These markers included specific dietary restrictions, observing the festivals, and circumcision. In both Romans and Colossians we find that Gentiles are under no obligation to become Jews, nor observe those things that were shadows of Christ. That said, Gentiles who wish to participate in Old Testament feasts are at liberty to do so as guests within the New Testament era and in the context of modern Messianic movements.

Our last text, Galatians 4:9-11b is also a significant text in our discussion of the feasts, "You observe days and months and seasons and years. I fear for you, that perhaps I have labored over you in vain." In this passage, Paul is critiquing those who were burdening Gentiles with becoming Jewish. Please note that the following is a simplified account of the Galatians discussion. Within the early church, believers viewed themselves as living within the realities of what feasts and Sabbaths promised and pointed towards. These realities were brought to the church via the person and work of Christ. For example;

the Sabbath was a day of rest from daily physical labors, but it ultimately pointed to the rest found in Christ which frees us from labors in regards to the spiritual. The reality of the Sabbath is found here and now in Christ, but would be ultimately realized in the eschaton. Theologians would famously coin this the "already/not yet" dynamic.

Another consideration on this topic comes from what occurred during the Jerusalem council in Acts 15. This council came together to discuss what was required of the Gentiles in relation to the law. The goal of this council was to keep the peace between Jews and Gentiles in the midst of a great shift in ethnic boundaries. Ultimately, the council put no requirements of feasts or diet upon the Gentiles with exception to that which pertains to blood.

A historical factor worth remembering consists of the details of the feasts that we laid out prior. For example; many of them required sacrifices or later developed pilgrimages which modern adherents are unable to observe. While Messianics partake in the feasts, they partake in a modernized version with no temple or sacrifices. This is not only because Messianics recognize that the substance has come, but also because it is impossible to re-create the feasts as they originally were observed. Those who place a burden on Christians to legalistically observe the feasts because they are the "biblical feasts," simply are not participating in the feasts the same way they were instituted in the text.

THE PASSOVER IN PARTICULAR

A big question has emerged in recent years about whether Christians should observe Passover. This is ultimately a matter of personal freedom as we find nowhere in the New Testament the expectations that Gentiles are expected to take on the Old Covenant festivals. When the church gathered and discussed the expectations of Jewish and Gentile relationships, there was no mention of obligatory Old Covenant holy days (Acts 15). Instead, Paul tells individuals to act in accordance with faith and conviction (Romans 14) and explicitly speaks to those in Colossae, saying, "Therefore let no one pass judgment on you in questions of food and drink, or with regard to a festival or a new moon or a Sabbath. These are a shadow of the things to come, but the substance belongs to Christ." (2:16-17).

While many with interest in the growing Hebrew Roots movement have pushed back against this text on this point, it is consistently made. It has always been understood as clearly referring to Jews, whether syncretistic or not, who would push obedience to Jewish law on Christians. Such issues are dealt with on equally important matters of Jewish identity, such as circumcision in Galatians, and the sentiment would be repeated in Romans 14. The passage in Colossians speaks to the law's dietary restrictions first, "food and drink." Gentiles were only told to abstain from meat that had blood remaining in it for the sake of the Jewish brothers and sisters in Acts

15. This is also addressed in Mark as well as Acts 10:14. Not only are the dietary restrictions indicated, but the issues of "festivals or new moon or a Sabbath."

While the observance of festivals and new moons was common in nearly every society, the inclusion of the Sabbath makes it clear that what is in view are the observances of the Jews. The Sabbath was distinctly Jewish, marking them from Gentiles and a key component of Jewish identity. James Dunn, in his commentary on the Greek text of Colossians,

> "The point is put beyond dispute when we note that the three terms together, "sabbaths, new moons, and feasts," was in fact a regular Jewish way of speaking of the main festivals of Jewish religion (1 Chron. 23:31; 2 Chron. 2:3; 31:3; Neh. 10:33; Isa. 1:13–14; 1 Macc. 10:34; Ezek. 45:17, and Hos. 2:11 in reverse order, as here; see, e.g., Sappington 163; Aletti, Épître aux Colossiens 193 n. 112). In view of later discussion we should also note that the Essenes claimed to have received special revelation regarding "the holy sabbaths and glorious feasts" and also the new moon (CD 3:14–15; 1QS 9:26–10:8). We must conclude, therefore, that all the elements in this verse bear a characteristically and distinctively Jewish color, that those who cherished them so critically must have been the (or some) Jews of Colossae, and that their criticism arose from Jewish suspicion of Gentiles making what they would regard as unacceptable claims to the distinctive Jewish

heritage without taking on all that was most distinctive of that heritage."[1]

Dunn is helpful on this point as well,

"That circumcision is not also mentioned is puzzling, but the issue clearly lay in the background, and the silence here may be sufficiently explained if the Jewish posture overall was more apologetic than evangelistic (see on 2:11). In contrast to those who think the absence of any mention of the law is a decisive impediment to identifying the Colossian philosophy too closely with a traditional Judaism (so Lohse, *Colossians and Philemon* 115–16 n. 11; Martin, *Colossians and Philemon* 91), it should be noted that circumcision, food laws, and sabbath were recognized by both Jew and Gentile as the most distinctive features of the Jewish way of life based on the law (cf., e.g., Justin, *Dialogue* 8:4; see also p. 33 n. 39 above).[9] And those who think the link with "the elemental forces" likewise diminishes the case for seeing traditional Jewish concerns here[10] need simply recall the same link in Gal. 4:9–10."[2]

Paul argues that the Old Covenant observances pointed to the reality that is found in Christ and that Christians are not under the Mosaic code (see also Romans 6:14-15; 2 Cor. 2:4-18; Gal. 3:15-4:7). The dietary laws, festivals, holidays, and sabbaths were fore-shadowing Christ and that Christians are not expected to live in those shadows. Such a distinction has been made appropriately by Christians for centuries.

Those who want Christians to observe Passover differ in how important these Old Testament observances are. Some range from making it completely obligatory, while others call it a personal preference that can bless the lives of the Christians by making them more Old Testament literate. While the latter has its merits and is commendable, the former, sadly, is the attitude of many infatuated with the new movement. Addressing that position in particular, the approach has been found erroneous by Jews and Christians alike. The former critique these individuals (especially evangelical Gentiles pushing these observances) for appropriating key markers of Jewish identity found in the Exodus. Not only this, but also because of the Passover Seder's development independent from Christianity. Christianity Today put out an interesting piece that can be critiqued in its own right, but which correctly points out that the Seder meal, as it is known today, was developed following the destruction of the Temple in Jerusalem and thus after the birth of Christianity.[3]

This isn't a new idea either but can be found in various literature such as Biblical Archeological Societies' Article on the subject. However, the article takes a low view of scripture and pits the Gospels against one another.[4] While the Biblical Archeological Societies' article disagrees with myself and many scholars with a high view of scripture, it points out some of the issues I have mentioned above. Passover had sacrifices, Passover had a pilgrimage to Jerusalem, and what it looked like in Jesus' day is hotly debated. While Jews commemorate the Passover and the Exodus, they do so in a modified form that developed after Christianity's inception, and, because of those missing elements of the 1st century, such as the priesthood and temple, it is never observed as the Jews initially observed it.

The points are simple: firstly, modern Passovers are modifications, not the same Passover that Jesus observed. Even the system of dating the Passover has changed since Jesus' day. Secondly, Passover, as it was developed, was developed alongside Christianity. This means it makes little sense for a Christian who is Gentile to partake in a later-developed Jewish festival formed independently from Christian practices.[5]

Shane Morris, in his article responding to the piece by Christianity Today, critiques the article but adds this qualification,

"I would ultimately not participate in any kind of religious or liturgical observance of the Passover Seder (as opposed to artistic or pedagogic observances, which I see no problem with.) Grasping the true relation between Judaism and Christianity is important. But it's even more important, if you're a Christian, to get your own religion right. And contra Messianic Jews and Hebrew Roots adherents, Christian theology has historically held that Old Testament rites, including the Passover meal, have been replaced by New Testament rites. The two main sacraments of the Hebrew religion (Passover and circumcision) have given way to the two main sacraments of Christ (baptism and the Lord's Supper), which the New Testament explicitly links to the Jewish rites (1 Corinthians 5:6-8, Colossians 2:11-12).

In other words, Christians should not celebrate any form of Passover Seder in our worship because Christ replaced the Passover meal with His own body and blood, and has not authorized us to revert to the old (which the book of Hebrews, appropriately, calls "types and shadows of the good things to come"). Eating a Passover Seder in a Christian church is the equivalent of returning to circumcision or sacrificing bulls and goats. It is a reversion from the fulfilled reality, to the unfulfilled shadow. And though Christians have every right to consider the Exodus and all it represents our own, we believe we have what the "night different from all other nights" ultimately prefigured. Christ, as Paul wrote, is "our Passover Lamb." On the cross He gave us the unleavened bread of His body, the wine of His blood, and the sweat of His brow. Why would we return to sheep and bitter herbs?"[6]

This articulation by Morris is not only defended in the New Testament in various instances, particularly in Hebrews, but the position of Christians for centuries. Instead, Christians have made their own festivities to celebrate exclusively Christian realities. Whether or not one agrees with that and wants to participate in it is a matter of conscience and debate. Christians should not force the Old Covenant upon Christians, in this case, Passover. If the argument is, "Jesus did it, and so will I," then you should be held to that in observing the law in all respects. If one is unwilling to go so far, they should be at least held to observe the Passover as Jesus would have minimally with a pilgrimage to Jerusalem.

On the flip side, no Christian should force Easter (see part four for the connection between Easter and Passover) on another Christian. Ultimately, no holiday is binding on another Christian, and all Christians who observe any day must do so in faith; otherwise, it is a sin. From here, a personal study of Romans 14 should be conducted as you weigh and measure the issue of Easter and other Christian-instituted holidays. To the question as to whether or not it is permissible to have holidays that are not established in the text of scripture, we can address that briefly.

Usually, Passover comes up in relation to Easter. It is argued that Easter shouldn't be observed at all, and it becomes a matter of individuals needing proof texts or a specific command to observe a day for the resurrection. Still, in many cases, the assumption at play is that an annual celebration not explicitly commanded in scripture is forbidden. Of course, this is problematic when applied to Easter, which can be summarized in this point: most Christians, including critics of Easter, will, and have, conceded that celebration of the resurrection is ascertained from the New Testament, a fulfillment of the Passover, and this celebration is done when the assembly gathers to worship God. Why is this a problem? Because they have already conceded that commemorating the resurrection is permissible, going a step further and saying so is an annual focus on the event is difficult to deny.

THE SUBSTANCE IS CHRIST AND APPLICATION

*I*n light of this fact that the substance of these feasts are found in Christ, we find the early church establishing new, or Christocentric, festivals. Not long ago I was asked why I don't celebrate Passover. Christians do celebrate it in one sense, but only in regards to Christ's death, burial, and resurrection. Noting how closely tied all these feasts are, it is worth remembering that for Christians, every Lord's Supper we take is a type of Passover meal. It is when we recognize the perfect Passover lamb. Resurrection Sunday[1] supersedes the feast of First Fruits in Christian tradition as well. In regards to the Passover, every partaking in the Lord's Supper is ultimately a remembrance of the better Exodus found in Christ who is the better lamb. There is a recognition here by the New Testament authors that the Passover was practiced differently now. Now the church would 'eat the lamb' at the Lord's supper while recognizing Jesus as the lamb. Resurrection Sunday is related to the Passover, but also the feast of First Fruits. This too is realized in Christ as "Christ has been raised from the dead, the first fruits of those who have fallen asleep." (1 Cor. 15:20). Paul also notes in verse 23, "but each in his own order: Christ the first fruits, then at his coming those who belong to Christ." Christians celebrate this feast, but in the reality of Christ and his work on Resurrection Sunday. While Messianics likewise recognize the significance of Christ in their celebration of events such as the Passover, differences can be seen in the when, how, and emphasis of their observances.

This concept of celebrating God's work revealed in Jesus can also be seen in holidays such as the feast of Nativity, which focuses upon the incarnation. Some have linked it to the feast of Tabernacles because Jesus came and "tabernacled" among us, but it's really a celebration of a miraculous work of God in bringing about the New Covenant. Just as the Jews formed Hanukkah to celebrate a miraculous work of God, Christians did the same by forming Christmas. The fact that Jews formed a cultural holiday on the basis of God's work is an important factor when considering holidays that celebrate things like the incarnation.

It should be remembered that when one says that they celebrate a biblical feast, they are really celebrating a modern version of it. The destruction of the temple in AD 70 caused the celebrations to morph significantly, since the sacrificial component could no longer be observed as it was in the Old Testament. The original feasts were significant for Israel, especially to counter a culture which revolved around an agricultural calendar that celebrated pagan gods as orderlies over the earth. It is important to note that holidays that mark seasons like Spring (new life) and Winter (darkness or light in the darkness) are almost universal across the globe because of how much the ancient world relied on agricultural events.

However, while a case has been made demonstrating that the feasts are not required of Christians, this discussion shouldn't lead us to see the Feasts as meaningless or burdensome. Instead they should be seen as a beautiful picture of God's plan of redemption and how God gave us the substance of these pictures and promises. The feasts can provide an opportunity for Christians who observe them to connect deeply to the Old Testament and realize the beauty of the Gospel. At the end of the day, Christians and Messianic are free to observe the feasts of the Old Testament if they desire. Just as well, Christians are free to not observe them. May we never become legalistic by enforcing our conscience onto others in regards to these issues, especially given that the New Testament authors wrote to this particular topic in the early church when divides were more strenuous between Jews and Gentiles. There's nothing new under the sun, so let's learn from that which came before us.

PART II
CHRISTMAS AND PAGANISM

INTRODUCTION

The discussion on the origins of Christmas are emotionally heated, convoluted, and often difficult to navigate. After spending hours in research, documentation, documentaries, and perspectives on various positions, I have found there is a great deal of conflicting information on the conversation. Because of this, I believe it would be helpful to briefly explain my methodology and sources used when putting together *Part 2: Christmas and Paganism.*

The sources I used for this section included numerous articles and journals on both sides of the discussion. In order to counteract confirmation bias to the best of my ability, I treated sources that supported my presuppositions with a higher degree of skepticism than those opposing my views.

One example of this can be found in a citation of Theophilus, who lived between AD 115-118. He was allegedly reported to have said, "We ought to celebrate the birthday of our Lord on what day soever the 25th of December shall happen." A lengthy search on this quote led me to discover it was found in a work of Rudolf Hospinian, rather than Theophilus. Because Hospinian wrote in a language I do not know, I was unable to survey his work and verify the quote's original author. I also found no reference to it when looking through Theophilus' accessible works. Ultimately, I had to conclude there was not enough information to use the citation in this argument.

Another argument in defense of a historical celebration of Christmas claimed that a bishop had instituted services on Christmas eve in the 2nd century. However, there was too little evidence to be usable.

In addition to journals, I searched through encyclopedias, dictionaries, and pre-Nicene (325) early church Writings. I consulted two documentaries that were anti-Christmas, and three videos that were pro-Christmas – one Lutheran, one Eastern Orthodox, and one Roman Catholic.[1] While examining this topic, I found that a good number of protestant sources were content to accept the narrative that Christmas was simply a way of Christianizing a pagan holiday. This notion could likely be traced back to the Protestants who lived during the Reformation. The Puritans would even ban and outlaw Christmas on the same basis laid forth by the anti-Christmas crowd today. In the sources section of the notes you'll find some Eastern Orthodox websites, as well as a Catholic website I used to access early church documents.

As I have researched the topic, I humbly recognize the difficulty of the historical puzzle laid before us. The discussion has many facets and factors that must be considered in order to put together a complete picture. I must point out that there are intelligent men and women whom I deeply respect on both sides of this debate. Thus, I am obligated to say that in this part of the book, this is my interpretation of the data, history, and circumstances. Ultimately, "Each one should be fully convinced in his own mind" (Rom. 14:5b) in regards to whether or not they "esteem one day as better than another."

The question we are seeking to answer is simple: "Is Christmas pagan?" Yet, what many are actually asking is, "Are the *roots* of Christmas pagan?" The answer to this is "no," when Christmas' *original* design and focus is considered. *This needs to be stressed:* Even if Christmas turns out to replace or Christianize a pagan holiday, its purpose, function, and role is categorically Christian, regardless of how we feel about Christianization of elements.

If the question posed was, "Is Christmas pagan *now* in terms of how it is practiced?" the answer would still be "no," because most of the world population is not pagan according to the actual definition of paganism. However, if we asked "Is Christmas *secular* now?" we could affirm this quite heavily, but in terms of contemporary practice, not in its fundamental origin and purpose. The problem for Christmas is not paganism, it's secularism (see also chapter 16, "Cheap Paganism" on defining paganism).

THEOLOGICAL/WORLDVIEW PRESUPPOSITIONS

It is necessary to begin the discussion on Christmas and Paganism by outlining my presuppositions, which are determined by a biblical worldview and theological truths found in scripture. The first theological presupposition is that the world will always attempt to subdue Christianity. This needs to be remembered when we are faced with rhetoric put forth by groups outside of Christianity such as Wiccans, Atheists, and Jehovah's Witnesses. In many cases, these individuals would gladly utilize whatever information is available that espouses the "Pagan roots of Christmas" to "crush" Christianity. The truth is even if we could prove without a doubt that Christmas had no tie to paganism in any shape or form, it would be rejected with 'evidence' to the contrary simply because of the theological reality that the world wants nothing to do with Christ.

For example: If you talk to a Jehovah's Witness or many unbelievers influenced by the DaVinci Code about what Emperor Constantine did in the church at Nicaea, you will often hear a false narrative. This narrative claims that he created Christianity and the Bible, and is said with confidence as if it were an obvious fact. However, when faced with a plethora of evidence to the contrary, you'll see a happy acceptance of historical revisionism without basis. Although our conclusions need to be based on the evidence, we should still be mindful when a group of non-Christians collaborate on anti-Christian rhetoric.

The second theological presupposition is closely related to the first. This is the theological presupposition that sin and man will corrupt anything good. This can be demonstrated with the abuse of anything good – marriage, wine, strength, intelligence, and many others. For example, look at Christmas and the sudden inclusion of Krampus. He is Saint Nicholas' strange counterpart, who is part demon and drags children to hell for being naughty. Another corruption can be found in the moralism that is commonly promoted in the gift-giving narrative of the modern practice of Christmas. This is directly contrary to the message of grace and the Gospel.

The last theological presupposition is focused upon God's providence and his glory in the restoration of the world. How this comes into play will be discussed as we continue through part 2.

Before we dive into the historical data around Christmas, I want to briefly address one objection to the observance of the holiday. This will be further discussed in part 3, but is necessary to introduce at this point because of its prevalence.

A DETOUR

In this detour we will address the common argument that states "We shouldn't celebrate a holiday not found in the Bible." Our discussion on this will be brief for now, as it will be further examined in part 3, *"The Biblical Case for Celebrating Christmas."* The heart behind the argument is admirable, but there are several issues with it. To address this point, I will briefly look at two texts from scripture, a practice likely observed by Jesus, and point out a simple observation that is sometimes overlooked.

First, let us consider Colossians 2:16-17. In this text, Paul tells those in Colossae that they shouldn't let anyone judge or condemn them concerning festivals. Within this context, Paul is specifically speaking about Jewish feasts and the Sabbath. However, the application is easily trans-ferrable to any type of celebration. Celebrations do not make us more righteous or unrighteous on their own according to Paul. Obviously, if one is participating in sin that is prohibited in the scriptures during such celebra-tions, then an issue is present. With this principle in mind, many throughout church history have rightly condemned the tendency to indulge in sins such as glut-tony, while not condemning the celebration itself.

At the end of the day, what you do or don't celebrate has no bearing on your relationship to God so long as it is done in faith and unto the glory of God. Paul expounds on this more fully in Romans 14, where he specifically discusses festivals and the eating of meat sacrificed to idols.

Paul exhorts that you should not partake in a celebration if it goes against your conscience, because it would be a sin. Paul links this principle to faith and says, "The faith that you have, keep between yourself and God. Blessed is the one who has no reason to pass judgment on himself for what he approves. But whoever has doubts is condemned if he eats, because the eating is not from faith. For whatever does not proceed from faith is sin." (Rom. 14:22-23).

I would suggest conducting a study on Romans 14, but it should be noted here and now that if you leave this discussion not fully convinced that you should participate in the holiday, then don't. It would be a sin to do so. However, Romans 14 also notes that you should not judge those who have a clean conscience to partake in the holiday. Paul says that those who do partake in the holiday, while esteeming and honoring the Lord, are in good hands. At the same time, he says that the one who abstains for the Lord, in order to honor him, is also in good hands (v. 5-9). If one is torn on their proper course of action, it is better to abstain, research, pray, and assess the topic each year.

The second point worth addressing is the high probability that Jesus celebrated a holiday that was not found in the Bible. It was even a winter holiday, which was established during the intertestamental period. This festival was known as the feast of Dedication, otherwise called Hanukkah. The feast of Dedication commemorates an event that occurred around 165 BC. This means that this celebration is not only lacking biblical justification, but for Jesus and his contemporaries, this festival was a relatively new cultural celebration.

The basis for the feast of Dedication is the Maccabean revolt. A Syrian King invaded the Jewish nation and tried to force them to abandon God. He also brought in Greek customs and imposed them on the Jewish people. The climax of this conflict occurred when the invaders defiled the Temple by placing idols within it and making a sacrifice to a pagan deity on the altar. In response to this great insult, the Maccabees warred against the Syrians and drove them out. This feast commemorates the victory of God over the Syrians and deliverance of the people from their enemies. The holiday came about because a "great miracle happened there" (as traditions says). The time of light in the midst of great darkness is emphasized with the festival's other name, "the festival of Lights." Within the text of John 10:22-23, this festival is mentioned by name, and there is no rebuke for the observance while Jesus seemingly participates. As a Jew who is present and walking in the temple courts during the feast of Dedication, there is little reason to think that Jesus would not participate. In addition to this, Jesus had already boldly confronted people who misused the temple at this point in his ministry. The most relevant example to this discussion is Jesus' clearing of the temple courts in John 2:13-22, because of the defilement of sanctity and worship. In contrast, Jesus in John 10:22-23 does not have a rebuke for the festivities occurring, but instead the exchange is focused on the people's unbelief. It is worth pointing out that men of faith have differed on whether or not Jesus observed the feast of Dedication, though most commentators hold that Jesus participated. The grounds for this are found in the simple truth that Jesus, who was truly man, participated in human traditions within his cultural setting as one would expect.

This last point, which may not apply for everyone, is the reality that we observe other holidays and do many things that aren't explicitly noted in scripture. Arguing to abstain from that which is not found explicitly in the Bible is problematic and reductionistic, practically speaking.

THE POSITIVE CASE

$\mathcal{W}$ith preliminary considerations out of the way, we can begin our positive case. It seemed appropriate to present this view initially, and then raise reminders of these points later, against the criticisms of the negative case. However, I'd first like to point out that the two major critiques against Christmas actually depend on a *lack of data* from Christians prior to AD 274 and AD 350, which we'll call hinge dates. We will go into detail on these points as we proceed, but *what has to be true for these two criticisms to hold water* is that the date of December 25th was chosen because it was assimilated by Christians from pagans rather than being chosen independently from pagan celebrations. Another concept worth noting is that Christmas wasn't called this until much later - it was initially known as the feast of the Nativity.[1]

This is important to know when reviewing information, such as the 20,000 martyrs of Nicomedia, as sources typically describe Christmas as the feast of Nativity. Additionally, the feast of Nativity was not merely centered around the single day of December 25th, but rather was the start of a twelve-day period which ended during the feast of Epiphany on January 6th. The feast of Epiphany has early attestation, and was a feast that celebrated the public manifestation of Jesus at his baptism. As far as I'm aware, it is typical for eastern churches to continue this particular pattern. The west, however, places more emphasis on advent, which developed in the 4-5th century. Advent focuses upon the time leading up to Christmas day. As the church grew over time, the liturgical calendar grew as well, and would eventually encompass the entire year with set seasons and corresponding observances.

Within the early centuries of the church, Christians put a heavy emphasis on the nature of Jesus. Particularly relevant to our discussion was the church's focus on Jesus' humanity. A worldview known as Gnosticism led to a number of heresies, which denied the humanity of Christ. The early forms of Gnosticism can be detected in the apostle John's writings, who speaks heavily against those who deny that Jesus took on human flesh (cf. 1 John 4:2-3; 2 John 1:7). Because of this theological tension, an emphasis on the importance of the incarnation, Jesus' conception, and his birth from the virgin Mary quickly arose. While these discussions were quick to arise, the earliest historical source referencing December 25th as the birth of Christ dates from between

AD 200-211. This reference, however, is significant years prior to our earliest hinge date of AD 274. This source is often neglected in discussions on the subject, even by apologists. An early Christian writer, Hippolytus of Rome, has a commentary on Daniel which says,

"For the first advent of our Lord in the flesh, when he was born in Bethlehem, eight days before the kalends of January (December 25th), the 4th day of the week, while August was in his forty-second year, but from Adam five thousand and five hundred years. He suffered in the thirty third year, 8 days before the Kalends of April [March 25th], the day of preparation, the fifteenth year of Tiberius Caesar..."[2]

Here, Hippolytus claims that Jesus was born on December 25th and died on March 25th. The significance is apparent, and while this particular text was once seen as questionable, it has since been deemed reliable.[3] Although Hippolytus does not mention of the feast of Nativity by name, the text remains important. Hippolytus' link between Jesus' birth and December 25th demonstrates the significance and independence of the date apart from any alleged pagan assimilation. This is to say that even if Christians were wanting a festival for themselves in the midst of pagan events, they already had a significant date to base one on. This is obviously opposed to the notion of Christians adopting a pagan date and merely Christianizing it.

Here it is appropriate to explain the calculation of the

early church. They desired to know when to celebrate the Pascha, or Easter, which is the feast of the resurrection of Jesus. The discussions on Easter were far more pressing than the discussions on the feast of Nativity, especially since there was tension in the church regarding when it should be celebrated. In order to celebrate the resurrection, the church needed to determine the date when Jesus died.

There were various proposals for this date, with two major dates held as being the date of Jesus' death by the third century: March 25th in the west, and April 6th in the east. The birth of Jesus was calculated by a tradition,[4] which stated that a prophet would die on the same day he was conceived. If Jesus died on March 25th then he would have been conceived on March 25th. Likewise, if he died on April 6th he would have been conceived on April 6th. Both of these conception dates are significant when we consider the nine months of pregnancy. With simple addition we find that nine months from March 25th is December 25th, and nine months from April 6th is January 6th. Remembering that December 25th traditionally began the season with the Nativity, and January 6th ended the season with the Epiphany, both of these dates are significant.

Clement of Alexandria (c. AD 150-195), states in his work Stomata, "There are those who have determined not only the year of our Lord's birth, but also the day." This is important, as he points to others who have come before him having already calculating these dates. He goes on to produce a list of various dates for Jesus' nativity, baptism, and passion. Much of the text here is unhelpful, as he uses an Egyptian calendar that was utilized in Alexandria. There have been a number of discussions surrounding this calendar and Clement's proposed dates, but the general consensus is that taking the Egyptian calendar and corresponding it with the Roman calendar to come up with dates is a frequent, although problematic, practice.

The issue is based on the fact that the Egyptian calendar did not account for leap years. Regardless, Clement's work states that some individuals believed Jesus was born or conceived (as the term used could refer to either), in March, April, or May. When calculating Clement's statements, some interpreters have noted that he seems to indicate January 6th or November 18th as Jesus' birth. This work quickly becomes difficult to understand, as can be seen through the many interpretations and discussions surrounding Clement's Stomata. However, we can find some interesting food for thought if we look at the dates put forward.

If we take his March and April dates as the time which some believed Jesus to be "conceived," then Jesus' birth would be in December and January. I would suggest that this is reasonable, given the tradition noted previously, which placed Jesus' death and conception on March 25th or April 6th. Additionally, if Clement indeed holds to January 6th, this would still be relevant to the early Christmas tradition. This minimally tells us that Clement and the others he referenced were thinking about Jesus' birth long before our hinge dates. The dates put forward were calculated, rather than selected on the basis of surrounding pagan festivities. Some of those dates are relatively close to our contemporary understanding of Christmas. Not only were the dates put forward calculated prior to our hinge dates, but it seems the dates were selected based on these early calculations, independent of pagan influence. This is to say that the church held to these dates because they were already accepted tradition.

As mentioned above, Hippolytus's commentary is the only explicit mention of December 25th available until AD 386 with John Chrysostom's homily in Antioch.[5] John, a writer in the East, claims that the celebration of the feast for the birth of Christ is an ancient tradition, and he appeals to Roman tax records known of in the West. In the homily, he states that the 25th of December is the "day of the birth of our Savior Jesus Christ." Four points Chrysostom makes are:

1. December 25th, as the date of Christ's birth was known "from the beginning in the Western church."
2. Christians in his day were arguing about whether or not the day was accurate.
3. He gives three proofs for the December 25th date.
4. He never mentions any pagan celebration in his exposition. Instead, he appeals to scripture, history, and tradition.

The proofs Chrysostom mentions are as follows:

- The time of the census mentioned in Luke 2:1-7. He states that this census occurred in December.
- He points out that whoever doubts and wants to know the exact time of the census can search the ancient records, which were kept in public libraries in Rome. He implies that the time of Jesus' birth is easily verifiable.
- He argues from scripture, namely the timing of Zacharias' service, Elizabeth's conception, and the visitation to Mary, that these lead to a December calculation. He concludes that Elizabeth became pregnant in the latter part of September (after Tabernacles), and Mary became pregnant six months later in March. Nine months from that, and we have a December date.

Furthermore, in a collection of earlier Christian writings compiled between AD 375-380 known as the "Apostolic Constitutions," we read,

"Brethren, observe the festival days; and first of all the birthday which you are to celebrate on the twenty-fifth of the ninth month; after which let the Epiphany be to you the most honored" (Book V. Section 3).[6]

The same document again later states, "Celebrate the

day of the Nativity of Christ."[7] Further, this same document says about the pagans, "We may not join in their feasts, which are celebrated in honor of demons."[8] Replacement or assimilation seems unlikely, given the Apostolic Constitutions' strong statements. It is farfetched to say that Christmas was a means of replacing or Christianizing pagan feasts, when the document says to have nothing to do with pagan celebrations *and* to celebrate the Nativity of Christ.

It is worth remembering that the Apostolic Constitutions are a collection of *earlier* documents. This means that the dating of AD 375-380 is unlikely to reflect when the document was actually penned. In fact, some scholars date book V, the book cited above, to have been written as early as the 3rd century. In addition, for the statements to be penned and accepted, there had to be consensus by church leadership regarding the exhortations within the documents. This also points to an agreement earlier than the document's formation and dating. I chose the later date of AD 375-380 conservatively. Without knowing the precise dating of the document, we must still consider it along with other evidence.

Tertullian, who lived prior to our hinge dates between AD 150-240, speaks against a number of pagan festivals as was common for the early Christians.[9] One of these festivals that Tertullian spoke against was Saturnalia,[10] which will be discussed in more detail in a later section. Tertullian in several writings[11] notes the devotion of seasons, days, months, and years for the early church showing that fixed times and celebrations were observed in the early church. Worth mentioning for transparency is that Tertullian did state that it was improper for Christians to decorate houses like a Roman Brothel on days of festivities with greenery, branching laurels, wreaths, and lamps. Whether or not Christians were doing this is unknown, as Tertullian in effect says "we don't do this" rather than "stop doing it." While some have pointed to Tertullian as evidence that Christians adopted such practices for Christmas, I'm not convinced we can conclude that Christians hijacked pagan festivities. In regards to the practice Tertullian mentions explicitly, it is worth pointing out that brothels are not marked in our culture by greenery, nor are these things used in honor of any gods any more than a flower on a window sill is a dedication to a god.

Moving on chronologically, we reach AD 302. In Nicomedia, one of the regions which suffered much under the Emperor Diocletian, a number of Christians were locked in their church and burned alive while celebrating a Christmas Eve service.[12]Aside from the significance of a Christmas eve observance occurring during this time, the edicts that led to the fire should be noted. The "Great Persecution" revoked the legal rights of Christians, and sought to force them to comply with Roman religious practices. Other edicts called on them to offer sacrifices to pagan gods. Christian refusal to comply with these edicts led to the last and most severe persecution of Christians living within the Roman empire. If Christians were assimilating Roman celebrations, then the fire in Nicomedia would have been entirely unnecessary. I would suggest that this martyrdom occurred due to the observance of Christian tradition when Christians were called to comply with Roman practices. Further, I would point out that a known Christian gathering would be an opportune time for enforcing punishment.

Next, in AD 312, a sect of heretics in North Africa known as the Donatists broke from the church. While they separated from other Christians, they clung to the faith and practices as it had been understood in their time. This included the celebration of Christmas. Christmas being observed by the Donatists is significant when we consider their disposition and understanding of the Christian faith.

The Donatists argued that Christians must be faultless for their prayers to be effective and for ministry. They were heavily legalistic, and claimed that Christians must be absolutely pure and holy. They also stressed that their purity and holiness proved their faithfulness. Anyone who wavered under the threat of death was considered impure and not worthy of being members of the church. In addition to this, they considered themselves to be the only true church, and would not accept the baptisms or communion of other churches. Donatists were the ultra-legalists of the day, and yet they celebrated Christmas. Furthermore, Augustine[13] notes that the Donatists rejected Epiphany on January 6th, because they viewed it as a late invention. How could a group such as this, with their understanding of purity and legalism, so readily hold to Christmas while also rejecting the early attested feast of Epiphany?[14]

Next, we come to the Chronograph of 354,[15] which is a calendar that included a number of feasts. One of those included is the feast of Christmas (sections 8 & 9 of the Chronograph). It lists Christmas as an established observance and that is what needs to be stressed here - this calendar speaks of what was already established. Some try to say that the date of this calendar is the year that Christmas was instituted. This does not track logically, as an event would only be added if it was already an established and significant event at the time it was put in the calendar. Further, Beth Dunlop outlines the Chronograph specifically in relation to December 25th,

"Three parts of the Chronograph contain evidence for the recognition of December 25 in the liturgical and civil calendars of Rome. The first part of the document relevant to our question is the Fasti consulares, a chronological listing of the consuls of Rome, which interjects "Christ is born during the consulate of C. Caesar Augustus and L. Aemilianus Paulus on 25 December, a Friday, the 15th day of the new moon." The second part of the Chronograph that provides evidence for the December 25 is the Depositio martyrum, a calendar of the death dates of martyrs which begins with "Christ is born on the eighth of the Calends of January, in Bethlehem of Judea." If this line is authentic, it seems to provide evidence that an ecclesial commemoration of the Nativity had joined the celebration of martyrs deaths, which were considered as their birth into heaven. The third piece of evidence in the Chronograph, which is probably the most convincing and from which we can assign a terminus ad quem of 336 for the commemoration of December 25 in Rome, is the Depositio episcoporum, a calendar of the death dates of Roman Bishops from 255 to 352." The calendar begins on December 26, not mentioning the birth of Christ, but leading us to believe that December 25 had become significant enough to be the beginning of the Church year in Rome.[16]

This information, coupled with our other sources which point to an earlier practice of this feast, is compelling. One historical detail we must remember when compiling all of this information is that it wasn't until AD 313, with the edict of Milan, that Christians were allowed to 'freely be' in society. Prior to this edict, occasions of persecution and martyrdom left little room for open festivities. Because of this, a lack of documented festivals isn't surprising, given the threat of persecution such as the Martyrs of Nicomedia.

A final consideration is found in the middle of the fourth century. Ephraim of Syria, who lived between AD 306-373, wrote a series of liturgical hymns[17] for use during the celebration of Christ's birth. If we consider the time in which he lived and the Chronograph of 354, we have yet another source pointing to an earlier tradition. I would further argue that these occurred independently from each other based on the distance between Rome and Syria.

A last issue to address within the positive case is the

date of December 25th itself. Typically, the idea of Jesus being born in December is disregarded as nonsense. However, we have seen that individuals who lived closer to the time of Jesus didn't think of the December date as nonsense and nor should we. As it was stated above, early church figures such as John Chrysostom and Justin Martyr, even made reference to having access to the tax records from the Roman census mentioned in the Gospels. According to Chrysostom, these documents were publicly accessible in Rome. He additionally says that the December 25th date can be justified from these records. Justin Martyr doesn't make a reference to the Nativity or December, but does mention the records as well. The authenticity of these records and claims are nearly impossible to verify, but are nevertheless compelling, given the witness of multiple individuals.

One can find scholars who argue that Jesus was born anytime between December to July, but of these, we find two predominate theories about his possible birth date. The two main positions are that either Jesus was *conceived* in December, or he was *born* in December. Both are possible, but December plays a role in either case.[18]Additionally, both of these positions can be derived from the biblical text and historical context. Dating from the biblical text hinges on the timing of Zachariah's service in the Temple, Elizabeth's pregnancy, and John the Baptists' birth because of his age in relation to Jesus. Calculations based off of John the baptists' conception and birth ultimately lead to Jesus being either conceived or born in November/December. To summarize, contrary to common opinion, there's good evidence that the traditional view is *possible,* minimally.

Finally, people will make much of the sheep being outside during the winter in Luke's gospel. They will say something like, "Jesus couldn't have been born in December because the Shepherds and Sheep were outside, and it would be too cold for them." This isn't true, though, as Jewish sources note that sheep can be comfortable year-round in Bethlehem. The exception is during the day in summer months. The climate of Bethlehem is very similar to Florida or Arizona, where you can go out in shorts during the winter. There is also a special breed of sheep that even drop lambs in December. Alfred Edersheim, a Messianic Jew, wrote,

"There is no adequate reason for questioning the historical accuracy of this date. The objections generally made rest on grounds which seem to me historically untenable."[19]

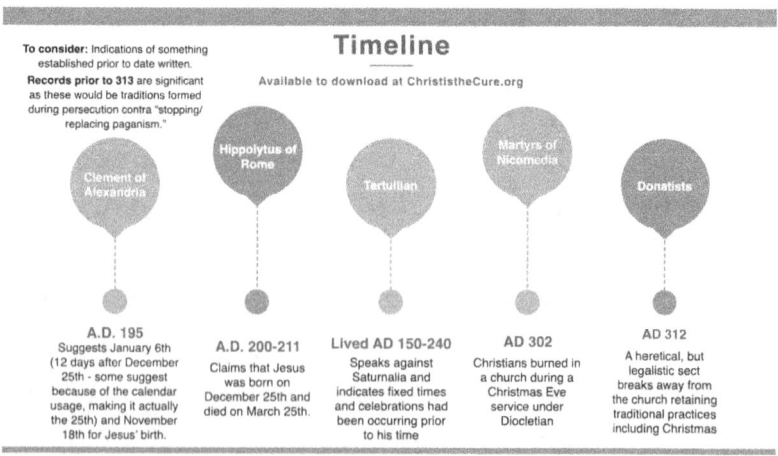

Timeline

To consider: Indications of something established prior to date written.
Records prior to 313 are significant as these would be traditions formed during persecution contra "stopping/ replacing paganism."

Available to download at ChrististheCure.org

Clement of Alexandria	Hippolytus of Rome	Tertullian	Martyrs of Nicomedia	Donatists
A.D. 195 Suggests January 6th (12 days after December 25th - some suggest because of the calendar usage, making it actually the 25th) and November 18th for Jesus' birth.	A.D. 200-211 Claims that Jesus was born on December 25th and died on March 25th.	Lived AD 150-240 Speaks against Saturnalia and indicates fixed times and celebrations had been occurring prior to his time	AD 302 Christians burned in a church during a Christmas Eve service under Diocletian	AD 312 A heretical, but legalistic sect breaks away from the church retaining traditional practices including Christmas

We can leave this part of our discussion by saying that the festival is ultimately celebrated on December 25th because of tradition and consensus of the early church. Additionally, it is a misunderstanding to think that the Eastern Orthodox Church doesn't celebrate on December 25th, as it is the beginning of their 12-day celebration. Many of those discussions center around which calendar is being used, which can become convoluted very quickly. It is my observation that many Eastern Orthodox adherents have stressed that they view December 25th as significant, and to say otherwise is to misunderstand their position.

ASSERTIONS AND ANSWERS

*I*t is now possible to address the various charges of paganism that the church has allegedly adopted. Individuals will frequently and arbitrarily blend pagan elements together, and make connections that don't logically or historically make sense. One example is the figure of Krampus, whom we mentioned earlier. Many articles and videos have used Krampus to show that Christmas is evil or pagan. The hidden assumption here is that Krampus was either always a part of the tradition and thus pagan, or that Krampus negates the Christian aspect because of its existence. The former can be proven historically false: Krampus was made as a counterpart to Saint Nicholas, at a much later date. To the latter assumption, the abuse of something doesn't negate its actual and original purpose. Another example is the condemnation of the celebration of Christmas due to our contemporary cultures' moralism narrative surrounding the holiday. Like with Krampus, this late addition to the celebration was not part of the original intention, nor does it negate the intention of Christmas. These examples demonstrate how many times elements are blended together without regard to history in order to push the narrative. This merging of arguments makes the topic more difficult to dissect, and one of the most common examples of this type of argumentation is found in the blending of ancient celebrations. Specifically, I'm speaking about the blending of Sol Invictus, Saturnalia, and the Winter Solstice together, and treating them as one unit. Contrary to this method of thinking, we're going to recognize them as individual celebrations and address them one at a time.

SOL INVICTUS

Of these three celebrations, the one most commonly brought up is Sol Invictus. The argument says that Christians adopted and replaced Sol Invictus, the feast of the Unconquered Sun. This point usually has a hidden assumption that anything pagan must necessarily precede anything Christian chronologically. Our theological presuppositions are key to remember here.

The claim is simple: Sol Invictus (the festival of the Unconquered Sun) was celebrated on December 25th, and Christians sought to replace the holiday with Christmas. In order to respond to this claim, we need to look briefly at the history surrounding Sol Invictus. The Historia Augusta speaks about the Emperor Marcus

Aurelius Antoninus, who ruled between AD 218-222. Aurelius viewed himself as a manifestation of the Syrian sun god. This is because sun gods were the most common of gods in paganism across the globe, and emperors in Roman culture were deified. According to the Historia Augusta (section 4),[1] Aurelius came to Rome and established himself as a god, built himself a temple, and declared that only he should be worshiped. According to this document, the Jews, Samaritans, and Christians were also to follow in this worship. Aurelius ultimately desired to establish a worship of Sol Invictus that assimilated *all* deities and their worship *including the practices* of Christians.[2] Unfortunately for him, his people assassinated him because of his ambitions.

About fifty years later Aurelian[3] came into power and ruled between AD 270-275. Aurelian attempted to re-introduce the worship of Sol Invictus by decree in AD 274. What is important to point out is that there is no record of the celebration being held on December 25th in AD 274. In fact, the traditional feast days of Sol were August 8th, 9th, 28th, and December 11th according to the early imperial fasti. He declared games dedicated to Sol would be every four years, but these games seem to have been held October 19th-22nd rather than any date near Christmas. Aurelian would eventually be assassi-nated by his officers as well.

Following these events, the Chronograph of 354 is created. This calendar not only contained a mention of Christmas, as we noted in the positive case, but also dates for Roman religious life. The Chronograph placed a festival for Sol Invictus on December 25th, but there is a small problem here - the entry has no mention of solis or sol. This entry only says "Invictus." Other entries related to sun God worship include "solis," like August 28th and October 19th-22nd.

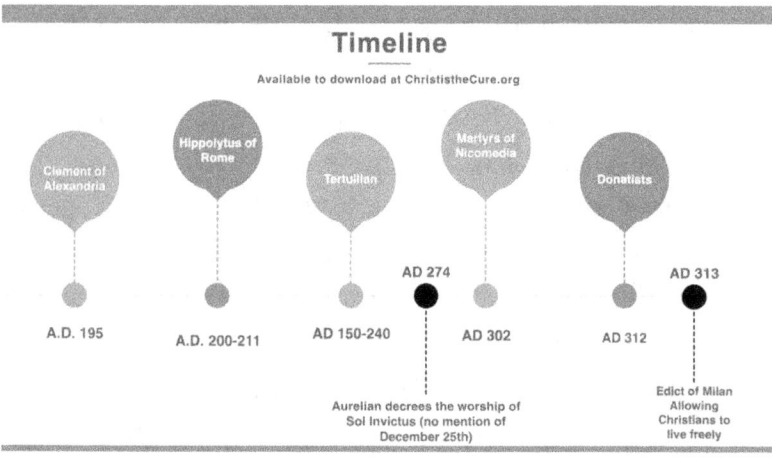

To summarize, Aurelian established a celebration for Sol Invictus (Sun Unconquered) in AD 274, but we have no record of a specific date. The calendar that has the alleged date of December 25th may or may not be related Sol Invictus as the terminology used makes it unclear. Yet, even if Aurelian did in fact place Sol Invictus on December 25th in AD 274, there is still a problem with the claim. I'll remind you now that 274 was one of our "hinge dates." Hippolytus, among other evidences for early tradition, pinned December 25th as the birth of Christ *prior to AD 274.* Given Aurelian's disposition towards Christians, it may have been a means to suppress a Christian holiday if he did indeed establish Sol Invictus on December 25th. Additionally, his vision may have lined up with Antonius' desire to assimilate other religious practices, which would have included Christian traditions.

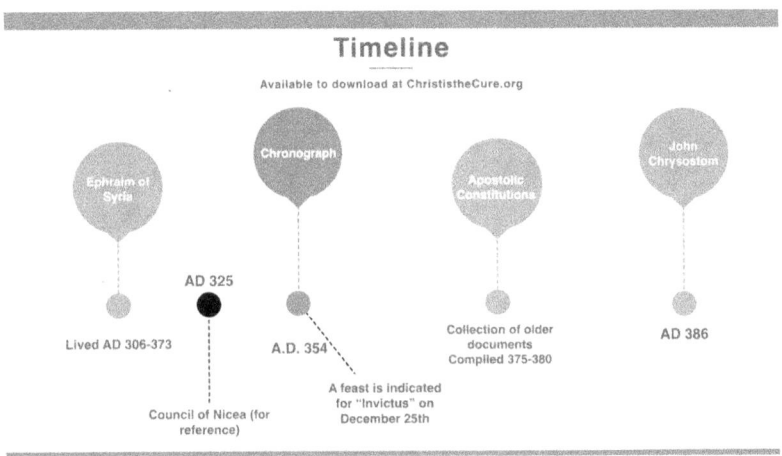

Because there isn't hard evidence of Sol Invictus celebrations in 274, we move into the first written date of the festival in 354. If we grant that the Chronograph of 354 places Sol Invictus on December 25th with certainty, it must be noted that on the calendar we find **both** festivals appearing. This is a simple point that needs to be stressed even if the evidence didn't point to an earlier celebration of Christmas. The idea that Christians tried to replace Sol Invictus doesn't track logically if both occur on the calendar at two separate times, especially when we take into consideration that Christians were known for staying away from Pagan celebrations historically up to this point.

WINTER SOLSTICE

Following Sol Invictus, a popular charge is that Christians merely chose December 25th because of the winter solstice. The winter solstice is the shortest day and longest night of the year, between December 20th and 23rd (the reverse is the case in the southern hemisphere). It is true that the winter solstice had been celebrated by pagans around the globe in many civilizations. In fact, it is difficult to find a culture that didn't celebrate around this time in December with corresponding symbols of fire or themes of light in the midst of darkness. The darkness corresponded with the darkest day of the year, and the light which would shine after this event was symbolic of coming out of that darkness. However, the solstice is simply recognized because of a natural phenomenon that is universally notable across human history. In many instances, individuals attempt to link all of the global solstice celebrations together, and conclude that Christmas is pagan – it's a winter celebration just like the others (see also chapter 17 in part 4).

The problem is first and foremost that solstice celebrations differed from each other. There also isn't evidence of Christmas being linked to these solstice celebrations. One could argue that the Christmas season is close to the solstice, but the latter revolved around sun worship and the natural phenomenon. In common rhetoric, geographical locations are completely disregarded as well. For example: the winter celebrations of the Incas or Norsemen are often said to have been ripped off by Christians, yet these societies were significantly distanced physically from early Christianity. Perhaps winter themes and traditions were later taken, but there isn't evidence of the establishment of Christmas being connected to the solstice. Another factor that is often disregarded is the tendency for pagans to assimilate cultures and be syncretists. It would hardly be surprising to find pagans converting to Christianity, adopting Christmas, and viewing old symbols in light of their new-found faith.[4] Regardless, I would conclude that the solstice was a phenomenon that was celebrated around the world because of prevalent sun worship.

A case study of how this looks could be seen in the celebration of Hanukkah. As mentioned prior, this observance occurred within this time frame of December, and also utilized the symbolism of "light," "fire," and "darkness" despite the holiday being centered around a historical event and not the solstice. It appears that they used symbolism common to the season of winter more than the solstice per se, in order to describe their perception of the historical events. The winter themes and symbolism used by many civilizations, even Jews during Hanukkah, would be easily transferable with the coming light of the world in the midst of hopeless darkness. Such language resonates with humanity and is even found in the Latin Vulgate's articulation of Job 17:12, "post tenebras spero lucem" (lit. After darkness, I hope for light). This saying would even be famously picked up as an axiom during the protestant reformation in the 16th century, "post tenebras lux" (Light after darkness). Just as there are common shapes throughout history that have taken on symbolic meaning, we should expect people to have similar ideas and expressions through language.

How do we respond to this information? First, it is worth remembering how Christians came up with December 25th. It was calculated by adding nine months to the day Christians held to be Jesus' death and conception. This is significant because it appears to be a mathematical conclusion, rather than a date based on a season or holiday. If there *was* any link to a holiday, it could have been linked to the Jewish festival of Lights as much as any pagan holiday.

Secondly, the winter solstice does not actually fall on the 25th of December. This is part of a larger discussion on calendar changes between the Julian calendar and the Gregorian calendar. In truth, the solstice would drift on the Julian calendar because of its poor calibration. Around Jesus' birth (estimated to be 3 BC), the solstice would have fallen around December 23rd. Additionally, the solstice would have fallen around December 20th at the time of the Chronograph of AD 354. There were two writers named Pliny and Columella, who would say that the solstice occurred *roughly* around the 25th, which would also allow for the 20th-23rd dates. Note in the image below how the solstice drifts *away* from the feast of Nativity's celebration of December 25th to January 6th. If Christians followed the solstice, we would expect the feast of Nativity to fall more within the solstice's actual occurrence. Instead, Christmas goes beyond December in the opposite direction. Even looking at our contemporary calendars, the winter solstice from 2016 through 2026 falls on December 21st or the 22nd with the former being the most common occurrence. If Christians were merely celebrating the winter solstice, surely, they could have done better in regards to their timing.

December

Available to download at ChrististheCure.org

Winter Solstice

Drifted on the Julian calendar (because of poor calibration) from the 23rd at Jesus' birth (est. 3 BC) and the 20th around AD 354

| 20th | 21st | 22nd | 23rd | 24th | 25th | 26th | 27th |

Feast of the Nativity

Began on the 25th and ran through until January 6th

| 20th | 21st | 22nd | 23rd | 24th | 25th | 26th | 27th |

SATURNALIA

Saturnalia is our next common charge against Christmas, which was a Roman festival of Saturn. Many will even mock Christians by saying, "Merry Saturnalia," thinking that Christmas is actually rooted in this pagan celebration. The problem with this argument becomes obvious when we look at the date of the festival, which was held on the 17th of December. The festival occurred over several days, and would eventually extend to around the 19th or 23rd of December. Remember, however, Christmas was initially practiced from the 25th of December to the 6th of January. I'd also remind the readers that in our positive case, we noted that Tertullian, an early church figure, spoke specifically against Saturnalia.

In general, information on Saturnalia is actually pretty minimal and ambiguous. Modern summaries of Saturnalia will often combine the various practices around the celebration from different regions, because the observance of Saturnalia differed based on where they occurred. Many link the exchange of candles and clay figures in some regions to Christmas, but it is difficult to say gift giving is pagan. As far as I've been able to ascertain, the tradition of gift giving at Christmas is linked to the 16th century. The practice came from Germany, and had a link to what is called the feast of Holy Innocents. In fact, the Germans had a major influence on American Christmas traditions, which will be brought back into the discussion later. The Christmas tradition of gift giving is a relatively new one that isn't necessarily linked to Saturnalia, nor does Saturnalia have an exclusive claim on gift giving. Gift giving is one of the oldest customs in humanity, regardless of seasons or celebrations. There is also a practice where those who participated in Saturnalia would go door to door naked while singing. While this is often said to be the basis for caroling, I'd like to point out that singing isn't inherently pagan,[5] nor have I ever seen Christians caroling in the nude.

Essentially, the argument is that there must be some kind of link between paganism and Christmas, but there isn't hard evidence to support this. Some will say that

Christmas trees, yule logs, holly, and ivy come from Saturnalia, but there is no evidence of those being involved in the pagan celebration. Yule Logs do seem to be linked to Norse holidays, but not Saturnalia. Just as well, burning a log in a fireplace is extremely common, especially during winter. Claiming this to be an exclusive pagan practice is peculiar, especially when we can find this tradition also in England during the 16th century. It is my perspective that the conclusion here is clear cut. The dates don't match up, and there isn't hard evidence for connections in regards to what was practiced during Saturnalia.

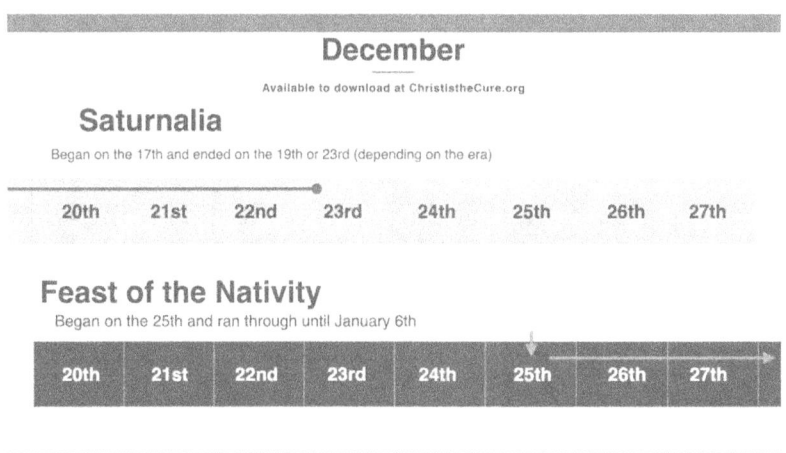

December

Available to download at ChrististheCure.org

Saturnalia

Began on the 17th and ended on the 19th or 23rd (depending on the era)

| 20th | 21st | 22nd | 23rd | 24th | 25th | 26th | 27th |

Feast of the Nativity

Began on the 25th and ran through until January 6th

| 20th | 21st | 22nd | 23rd | 24th | 25th | 26th | 27th |

PSEUDO-GODS

One of the most common charges against Christmas is built upon the notion of Christmas being the birthday of a pagan god, which was then adopted by Christians. We won't spend much time here, as these claims against

Christmas simply cannot be backed by evidence or original sources. Additionally, they have been refuted by many Christian apologists. The god Mithras is generally the most relevant, because there was a Roman cult linked to him while the other gods are sort of thrown together. How many gods will be brought into the mix varies, but what we find is that there isn't evidence for any of the common claims. Instead, we find the origins of many of these claims in pop culture like the movie Zeitgeist and online memes. This is similar to the Constantine myths found in the DaVinci code, which are now treated as common fact. Pick a handful of deities, couple them together, and you have a whirlwind of pseudo-history being championed as factual proof that Christians ripped off other religions. There are many resources that point out the lack of historical evidence for these claims, and so I would encourage you to perform some independent research. One book that does a fantastic job on the issue is J. Warner Wallace's "Person of Interest."[6]

Here we will briefly discuss one of the champions of these myths, because of the prevalence of his claims. In 1835, a Scottish minister named Alexander Hislop published a pamphlet called "The Two Babylons - Romanism and its Origins," in his zeal against the Roman Catholic Church. This work would impact the thinking of many religious groups, even cults such as the Jehovah's Witnesses. The idea he presented is that the Roman Catholic church was a disguise for ancient Babylonian religion. He handled "revolutionary" evidence, discussed claims about the origins of various 'popish' traditions, and attempted to connect them to ancient Babylonian religion. Most of his issues dealt with Christmas and Easter, but many have now recognized the fact that Alexander's work is a historical mess. There are conflicting opinions on whether he made up his claims or simply made connections based on vaguely similar sounding words. One of his more obvious historical blind spots is neglecting the celebration of Christmas in the Eastern church, which was not dependent upon Rome. If this interests the reader, you can search his name and find various treatments on the subject, one being Ralph Woodrow's article that is cited below.

One of the popular claims made by Hislop was that the ancient Mesopotamian god Tammuz (or Dumuzid) was linked to Nimrod, Noah's great-grandson. Hislop claimed that Nimrod married his mother Semiaramis, and had the child Tammuz,[7] who was allegedly born on December 25th. The way he draws this conclusion is by stating that Isis and Horus (Egyptian deities) were the same as Tammuz and his mother. Hislop states that Horus was born around the winter solstice. Thus, Tammuz was born on the 25th of December. Aside from the strange blending of Egyptian and Babylonian deities, if one were to look up Hislop's citation, they would find that he falsely said Horus was born around the winter solstice, when in fact it was Isis' older son Harpocrates. The celebration of Isis' delivery of Harpocrates was in the spring.[8] Woodrow notes, as a past supporter of Hislop's work,

"While seeking to condemn the paganism of Roman Catholicism, Hislop produced his own myths. By so doing, he theorized that Nimrod, Adonis, Apollo, Attes, Baal-zebub, Bacchus, Cupid, Dagon, Hercules, Januis, Linus, Lucifer, Mars, Merodach, Mithras, Moloch, Narcissus, Oannes, Odin, Orion, Osiris, Pluto, Saturn, Teitan, Typhon, Vulcan, Wodan, and Zoroaster were all one and the same. By mixing myths, Hislop supposed that Semiramis was the wife of Nimrod and was the same as Aphrodite, Artemis, Astarte, Aurora, Bellona, Ceres, Diana, Easter, Irene, Iris, Juno, Mylitta, Proserpine, Rhea, Venus, and Vesta."[9]

Despite the idea that Christians replaced the celebration of Nimrod and Tammuz, there's no historical evidence for the Nimrod and Tammuz claims, regardless of how popular they have become. What we find are the strange connections of Hislop being accepted without proper grounds (See also Appendix B).

CHRISTMAS TREES AND LOOSE ENDS

*I*n this chapter, we will discuss Christmas trees along with some miscellaneous topics. Around Christmas, there is always a heavy emphasis on the trees and how they are pagan, or at least a means to assimilate pagan practices. Jeremiah 10:2-4 is often quoted to support this assertion, and states,

> "Learn not the way of the nations, nor be dismayed at the signs of the heavens because the nations are dismayed at them, for the customs of the peoples are vanity. A tree from the forest is cut down and worked with an axe by the hands of a craftsman. They decorate it with silver and gold; they fasten it with hammer and nails so that it cannot move."

As mentioned, this passage is the common text used against Christmas trees. To refute this claim, we must remember that context is key. This text is about *fashioning an idol*. The craftsman worked with an axe, and the idol was polished with silver and gold. This isn't about a decoration, and it is erroneous to believe that idols were created by bringing a potted plant or a tree into your house. It is a negation of the historical and cultural context, and a misrepresentation of what an idol is, to suggest that Jeremiah is speaking against decorative greenery. There are numerous texts regarding lifeless idols (Jeremiah 10:5; Jeremiah 10:8-10). In fact, similar language is used in Isaiah 44:

> "Surely he cuts cedars for himself, and takes a cypress or an oak and raises it for himself among the trees of the forest. He plants a fir, and the rain makes it grow. Then it becomes something for a man to burn, so he takes one of them and warms himself; he also makes a fire to bake bread. He also makes a god and worships it; he makes it a graven image and falls down before it. Half of it he burns in the fire; over this half he eats meat as he roasts a roast and is satisfied. He also warms himself and says, 'Aha! I am warm, I have seen the fire.' But the rest of it he makes into a god, his graven image. He falls down before it and worships; he also prays to it and says, "Deliver me, for you are my god." (Isaiah 44:14-17).

These "trees" that were fashioned as idols (gods) had a specific function, and those who cite the passage loosely, do it with ignorance. In the Ancient Near East, a god had to approve and initiate the manufacturing process of its idol.[1] At the end of the process, special ceremonies and rituals were performed to allow the god to inhabit the idol and receive its tribute of food, drink, incense, etc.[2] Worship was centered around idols in the ancient world, and the idol was a means of communication from the deity to the people, and mediating worship from the people to the deity. According to idol makers, idols were animated by a divine essence. They were not just a representation, but a manifestation of the god's presence.[3] Wood was the most common material used, as it was significantly easier to fashion and readily available. Speaking about the 2nd commandment of the Decalogue and the fashioning of images or idols, Gentry and Wellum state,

> "the command has to do with images used as mediators of the presence or revelation of deity from god to human, or mediation of the worship of people to the deity. As Walton observes, 'The prohibition of images excluded in particular that sort of worship that understood cultic rituals to meet the needs of the deity through the image.'"[4]

Daniel Block spends some time discussing the fashioning of idols from the ancient idolater's perspective in his work on a biblical theology of worship. He first notes that the physical object was thought to become a god in essence.[5] Additionally, the production of the idol involved both the deity and human.[6] Block states that the "ordinary piece of wood or stone was transformed into an idol animated by the spirit of the god it represented."[7] The passage of Isaiah is relatable to our modern mind, as Isaiah points out how absurd it is that someone would take the same object he uses to build a fire to also make a god to thank for the fire.

If you are forming your tree by approval of a false god, performing rituals so a divine essence can inhabit the tree, and using the tree as a mediator, then yes, your Christmas tree is pagan. Otherwise, it's a tree. Theologically, it is no different from a potted plant. We have to respect the context. What is an idol? How does an idol function? Is a decorative item an idol? Do Christians regard a tree the way idolaters noted in Jeremiah and Isaiah would? The answer to all of these questions is a resounding no. Those who quote Jeremiah in this way are twisting the text for their conviction, whether they mean to or not.

So where did the Christmas tree come from? In numerous civilizations, Evergreens were viewed as symbols of life in the midst of the darkness of winter. This makes sense, as they remain green while many other plants fail to survive. Romans, Vikings, Druids, and many other cultures used evergreens to decorate for differing purposes. Common use of an idea doesn't automatically make something pagan or an idol. Trees are just trees. People will try to argue that because a tree or an egg was a sign of fertility for pagans, we should avoid it. If we apply this logic across the board, we find ourselves unable to interact with many things because pagans used them. This would include trees, stones, toothbrushes, toilet paper, and a nearly endless list of objects in the natural world. Should we be disallowed to draw pyramids in math class because of their notorious use in paganism? Absolutely not. The biblical model shows that God prevails over idols, and is over natural materials fashioned into idols as creator. Examples of this include the concept of circumcision, which was practiced in Egypt before Israel, and Paul with the unknown idol in Acts.

The origin of the Christmas tree is mostly linked to 12th century Germany, although a version can be seen in the 8th century. Germans considered December 24th a feast day for Adam and Eve. They would put on performances called "paradise plays," which told the story of Adam and Eve's expulsion from the garden of Eden. One of the props featured in the play was the paradise tree, made from an evergreen and decorated with apples. There are references to a tree in the 14th and 15th centuries,[8] but information is scarce. The most popular explanation of the tree's common use begins with a legend surrounding Martin Luther. The story is so popular that he is often credited as being the first to bring a tree into his home. The legend says that Luther was walking one evening while trying to compose a sermon, and saw so many bright and shining stars through the branches in the forest that he was filled with awe. He decided to try to recreate the feeling for his family by bringing an evergreen into the home and attaching candles to the branches. Whether or not this event actually occurred is unknown, but it has become a popular tradition that is repeated in various sources.

By the 1550s, Christmas trees were integral to German tradition. They would decorate trees with nuts, apples, paper flowers, roses, wafers, gold foil, and sweets. The tree would usually be topped with baby Jesus in a cradle or a star. Eventually, glass blowers would blow ornaments in the shape of nuts and apples and they would be placed upon the trees. Emigrants would export the tradition with them in later years, with varied reception. While some gladly incorporated the tradition, others completely rejected the Christmas tree, such as the Puritans in 1621. From 1830 to 1890, the tree became more common in public displays, with ornaments still imported from Germany. In the 19th-20th century, the United States moved from thinking of the tree as being German to being a generic Christmas tradition. Some suggest the shift was to make the holiday more family-centric and focused on gift giving. Some suggest that Queen Victoria was the primary cause of the tree being popularized, because she was featured in an image with one by the Illustrated London news.

LOOSE ENDS:

- **Santa Claus:** Contrary to the claims of the misinformed, Santa Claus was an actual person, and is not a distraction from the real meaning of Christmas. He was a fourth century bishop in Asia Minor, named Saint (st.) Nicholas of Myra. He suffered for Christ under the persecution of Diocletian, and is remembered today by Orthodox Christians for his charitable, compassionate, and Christlike life. Given their view on saints, reformers didn't particularly care for the St. Nicholas Tradition. Luther didn't like the tradition of St. Nicolas and wanted to make Christmas focused on "Christkindl," meaning "Christ Child." This term ironically morphed over time into Kris Kringle. Cultural changes, reinventions of the story, and passing time transformed the story of St. Nicholas into Santa Clause. Much of the modern 'Santa' is disconnected from his source, and the legend has been twisted and abused, just as other elements of Christmas.
- **Stockings:** The hanging of stockings over the fireplace is derived from one of the legends of the activities of St. Nicholas. The story says he left several gold coins in the stockings hung

over the mantle to dry of several poor young girls who were in desperate need of money.

- **12 days of Christmas:** The often misunderstood 12 days of Christmas represent the 12 days from the Nativity of Christ on the 25th of December to the baptism of Christ on January 6th, traditionally speaking. We discussed that briefly, but that is where it originated from. The song with the same title has an origin that is less clear, as there is a good deal of conflicting information surrounding where it came from and what it is meant to represent.
- **Nativity scene:** The display of a Nativity scene was popularized by Francis of Assisi beginning in 1223. However, images can be found of the Nativity prior to this, with all the elements of the biblical account placed into a single image.
- **Caroling:** Caroling door-to-door likely began in the late Middle Ages as a development from the earlier Christian practice of singing hymns and performing liturgical dramas on Christmas eve.

CONCLUSION

*I*n conclusion: is Christmas pagan? I would contest it is not, when we examine all the details and evidence. What we find are similarities in cultures and traditions across the world, but I would be so bold to say that this is no different than things such as using the stars for navigation, which is found independently in various cultures. Phenomena like this are interesting, but they don't mean that a feast specifically made for the purpose of celebrating the birth of Christ is pagan. Should you celebrate Christmas? That is up to you and your conscience according to Romans 14. Some thoughts that come to mind are these: the threat to Christmas is not paganism, but secularism. Aside from the bombardments of these types of claims against Christmas, we must recognize the influx of materialism and lack of focus on Christ. If we are going to celebrate Christmas and say that it isn't secular, then we need to actually celebrate it as it was intended. When it comes to the cultural elements, those are discussions that each family will need to navigate on their own. Not all cultural aspects are bad, which is important as we remember that even Jesus lived and operated in a particular culture. Here we are left to exercise biblical principles and apply them to our lives.

We should also remember that the date is of no consequence. We're heading the wrong direction when we say, "Christ wasn't born on December 25th," because it assumes we're *just* celebrating a birthday rather than the theological reality of the incarnation and the good news of God. Yes, they are linked, but we're celebrating the coming of the incarnate Son sent by the Father. December 25th is ultimately a long held traditional date. There is nothing wrong with such traditions so long as they don't contradict scripture. Additionally, pagans don't own the material world, our God does. He owns this world and everything in it. Pagans and secularists have zero claim on anything natural in this world, whether marriage, gender, or greenery. Our God is the God over creation, and Christians have always used symbols as a means of remembering the work of God in their lives.

A final thought is the contrast of the pagan world and Jesus' incarnation. While Romans may have celebrated the "Unconquerable Sun," Christians celebrated the conquering Son, who is God over the sun. While winter festivals celebrate the coming light in a dark season, Jesus is the true light who came during a dark season of human history. It is difficult for me to ignore the potential providence in these 'coincidences.' Just as God showed his glory over the Egyptians and their gods with the plagues, part of me wonders if it applies here as well.

To conclude, Philip Schaff, a church historian who admittedly takes the position that Christmas could probably have been a transformation or regeneration of pagan festivals,[1] notes the themes above mentioned by early church writers such as Chrysostom, Gregory of Nyssa, and so on. Schaff states,

"Finally, the church fathers themselves confirm the symbolical reference of the feast of the birth of Christ, the Sun of righteousness, the Light of the world, to the birth-festival of the unconquered sun, which on the twenty-fifth of December, after the winter solstice, breaks the growing power of darkness, and begins anew his heroic career."[2]

Schaff's summary of the Christmas festival is as follows:

"The Christmas festival is the celebration of the incarnation of the Son of God. It is occupied, therefore, with the event which forms the centre and turning-point of the history of the world. It is of all the festivals the one most thoroughly interwoven with the popular and family life, and stands at the head of the great feasts in the Western church year. It continues to be, in the entire Catholic world and in the greater part of Protestant Christendom, the grand jubilee of children, on which innumerable gifts celebrate the infinite love of God in the gift of his only-begotten Son. It kindles in mid-winter a holy fire of love and gratitude, and preaches in the longest night the rising of the Sun of life and the glory of the Lord. It denotes the advent of the true golden age, of the freedom and equality of all the redeemed before God and in God. No one can measure the joy and blessing which from year to year flow forth upon all ages of life from the contemplation of the holy child Jesus in his heavenly innocence and divine humility."[3]

PART III
A BIBLICAL CASE FOR CELEBRATING CHRISTMAS

INTRODUCTION

Our discussions thus far have been heavily centered around refuting objections to celebrating Christmas based on alleged pagan roots and traditions. This was the predominate focus because the main thrust of anti-Christmas rhetoric focuses upon these claims. However, even if we eliminate the claims of pagan origins, objections often persist against the practice of Christmas on the grounds that it is not celebrated in the Bible. As I began contemplating the notion that celebrating the incarnation is unbiblical because it is not explicitly taught in the Bible, I found it to be deficient on both a logical and biblical basis. To address this issue, we'll examine a few concepts. First, we'll discuss traditions of men, then look at celebrations in a broad sense, and lastly, turn to the incarnation in scripture.

While some may comment that the case made so far has lacked biblical support, the reason for this is that we have been discussing *historical issues* more than *exegetical issues*. It is when those charges are addressed that often the goal post is shifted to, "The Bible doesn't say to celebrate Christmas." Because of this shift in argumentation, I hope to demonstrate biblical support for celebrating the incarnation of God without having an explicit command to do so. Additionally, to say that the church cannot celebrate a miraculous work of God because he didn't command us to do so is an odd stance to take.

In order for this section in the Christmas discussion to be meaningful, I simply ask the reader to begin with a clean slate regarding their presuppositions on the alleged pagan origins of Christmas. I would even suggest ignoring the history of Christmas altogether, and focus only upon the Bible. With this as the starting point, I hope to make a case for celebrating this work of God without needing an explicit command to do so. As noted in the other sections, this discussion ultimately boils down to conscience and liberty, and for that I would recommend a study of Romans 14. Before moving on, it may prove helpful to define an important term, namely "incarnation."

Incarnation is a term that literally means taking flesh. It comes from the Latin text of John 1:14, "the Word became flesh and dwelt among us." Thus, the term came to fully encompass the doctrine of the eternal person of the Son adding to himself a human nature. A fundamental concept regarding the incarnation is that the human nature of Christ is not a person, but is a nature assumed by the person, the divine Son. In addition, Jesus the eternal Son still possesses his fundamental divine nature, but assumes a human nature and acts through it. The scriptures note that the Son became flesh, taking on the form of a servant voluntarily. Christ lived as a man, in thirst and hunger, while also living perfectly under the law in righteousness to fulfill what was required of humanity. The celebration of the birth of Christ is, first and foremost, intrinsically linked to the celebration of the incarnation. The incarnation is realized in the eternal divine Son miraculously being birthed as a human baby boy. With this definition set, we can speak to the topic of celebrations and traditions of men.

ADDING TO THE COMMANDMENTS OF GOD?

The polemical rhetoric goes like this, "Nowhere does God speak of making Christmas a part of Christianity, nor does he say to celebrate the Son's birth. It is a celebration that is created by men and thus we are disobeying God by adding to the commandment of God and partaking in the traditions of men." At times, this argument may be modified by excluding the phrase "adding to the commandment of God," because most will happily admit there is nothing obligatory, effectual, or salvific about celebrating Christmas. I personally have yet to see Christmas added to the list of Christian ordinances for those who support the holiday. It is my observation that those who are anti-Christmas tend to give the celebration more spiritual weight in regards to the status of those who partake or abstain. Ironically, these individuals, who are loosely quoting Mark 7:8 to condemn the practice of Christmas, are using a verse that was directed towards the legalism of the Pharisees who added rules and regulations to scripture. Who is the legalist? The one who adds to the commandment of God and holds it over another's head. I would postulate this happens more often with those who hold to an anti-Christmas perspective. Their commandment is simple when you boil it down: if it isn't explicitly in scripture, you shall not partake.

The anti-Christmas rhetoric is ultimately a way to say that we shouldn't esteem one day or season over another. The times I have heard this said explicitly, it was followed by, "every day is a celebration of the incarnation and the Gospel." This is true, but it negates the value of annual, planned, and dedicated observations. Why not tell Israel that every day is a celebration of the Passover? Of course, the rebuttal would be that the Passover was commanded in scripture. Yet, by what biblical prohibition can you tell others to not esteem a day or season unto the glory of God? You can't because there isn't one. In fact, Paul says quite plainly,

> "One person esteems one day as better than another, while another esteems all days alike. Each one should be fully convinced in his own mind. The one who observes the day, observes it in honor of the Lord. The one who eats, eats in honor of the Lord, since he gives thanks to God, while the one who abstains, abstains in honor of the Lord and gives thanks to God. For none of

us lives to himself, and none of us dies to himself."
(Rom. 14:5–7).

It would be wise to emphasize Paul's phrase, *"each one
should be fully convinced in his own mind"* and for each individual to take this scripture seriously on this subject.

This conversation can quickly become a more
complex and controversial topic on what is often called
"the regulative principle of worship." Historically, this
principle has been interpreted in various ways with little
agreement or consistency from its adherents. However,
my goal is not to get into the weeds as to whether or not
a congregation vs. individuals can celebrate Christmas,
but rather to address more broadly what I perceive to be
a solid biblical case for celebrating the incarnation. Most
of the anti-Christmas rhetoric I have witnessed stems
from individuals who are not even acquainted with the
"regulative principle" and so I digress with that in mind.

Individuals will often hold to the presupposition that
"traditions" or "traditions of men" are all inherently
wrong. In light of this, determining what is deemed a
"tradition of man" and thus wrong, quickly becomes a
matter of subjectivism. The notion that all traditions are
inherently wrong is founded upon a misunderstanding of
the Bible, ignorance of church history, and a failure to
recognize one's own traditions. The question to answer
is not whether traditions are bad in and of themselves,
but rather if we are elevating our traditions to become
equal in weight to scripture and if they have become a
means by which to disobey God.

For example, in the context of Mark 7 the Pharisees were using 'authoritative' traditions to "void the word of God" (v. 13). The text is not about celebrating a miraculous work of God, which Jews and perhaps Jesus himself happily did with the festival of Dedication (John 10:22-23). One tradition that was present in Jesus' day, but is often forgotten, is the establishment of synagogues. They were formed in the intertestamental period, and became the primary means of congregational assembly for Jews. These community centers were never commanded by God, and yet were the very center of *worship* and *religious life*. Consequently, if we take the argument that all traditions are bad to its logical conclusion, then the Israelites and Christians would be in hot water based on the belief that any involvement in an event not explicitly stated in scripture is a sin and is voiding the word of God.

Continuing with the logic that Christians shouldn't partake in traditions, and practices not explicitly stated in scripture, we can see the domino effect that inevitably eliminates countless things from the Christian life. We do many things in our day to day that are not explicitly mentioned in scripture such as utilizing modern technology to serve and worship God. Most modern church services have small ecclesiastical, often called circumstantial, details[1] not found in scripture, as well as partake in events and cultural activities. Additionally, we celebrate a variety of things, all the time, without the direction of scripture. At this point the obvious needs to be stated, we cannot merely do whatever we want. There are indeed principles and prohibitions in scripture, but we need to recognize the freedoms we have to put into practice the former and obey the latter. Before I expand on the discussion of celebrations in a general sense, I want to properly touch on Mark 7. While there are numerous texts that are ripped out of context for anti-Christmas rhetoric (such as 1 Peter 1:18), the text most consistently used is Mark 7:1-13 which says,

"And the Pharisees gathered to him with some of the scribes who came from Jerusalem. And they saw his disciples that were eating bread with defiled hands, that is, unwashed. For the Pharisees and all the Jews did not eat unless they first wash their hands, holding to the tradition of the elders and when they come from the market place, they do not eat unless they wash, and there are many traditions which they observe, washing cups, copper vessels, and pots. And the Pharisees and the scribes asked him, "Why do your disciples not walk according to the tradition of the elders, but eat bread with defiled hands?" And he said to them, "Isaiah did well in prophesying concerning you hypocrites, as it is written, "this people honors me with their lips, but their hearts are far from me." In vain they worship me while teaching as doctrines the commandments of men. You leave the commandment of God and grasp the tradition of men." And he said to them, "You have a fine way of rejecting the commandment of God, in order to establish your tradition! For Moses said, 'Honor your father and your mother and the one who reviles father or mother surely dies. But you say, 'If a man tells his father or his mothers, corban, whatever is given is corban you no longer permit him to do anything for his father or mother, while voiding the word of God by your tradition which you handed down. And many such things you do."[2]

When studying any text, we must always begin with looking at the historical and cultural context of the passage. There's a couple of things worth noting regarding the context of Mark 7. First, the traditions referred to in this text are customs developed by scribes in their interpretation of the law, which included the washings of various vessels and hand washing prior to eating. These customs were for the sake of ritual purity. Immediately we can see that the tradition of Christmas isn't comparable to these traditions. Those who choose to celebrate the holiday do not include Christmas in their interpretation of the law and they do not add it upon the law as a requirement. In addition, there is no claim of higher religiosity or "cleanliness" for partaking in the holiday by those who are pro-Christmas as there was with the scribes and the Pharisees in Mark 7. On the contrary, it is actually the anti-Christmas rhetoric that interprets the law to prohibit celebrations and implies that you are of higher religiosity for abstaining from such holidays.

Continuing through the text, Jesus presents an example of a tradition that is used by the Pharisees to reject a commandment of God, specifically the fifth commandment to honor one's father and mother by claiming "corban." Corban[3] is a term which indicates that something is being dedicated to God and shouldn't be used for anything else. This "corban provision" could be used as a loophole so that an individual didn't need to financially support their father or mother. This would be accomplished by deeming their money as corban, dedicated to God.[4] By bypassing their responsibility to care for their parents, they dishonored them, and broke the fifth commandment. The weight of the text is placed upon Jesus' citation of Isaiah 29:13 where he notes that the prophet spoke of these hypocrites who were leaders that rejected God and his will.

The issue is *not* that tradition is bad. The theological issues that are central to this text in Mark are regarding traditions being elevated over and against the commandments of God in such a way that the scriptures are "void." Tradition becomes a problem if it is used as a means of voiding scripture. By quoting Isaiah, Jesus is stressing the focus upon the heart in juxtaposition to mere external purity. Isaiah's audience said the right things, but they did not have a heart for God. They made themselves gods by creating traditions which supplant God's commandments.

It is here where I would postulate three ways we know that those who are in favor of Christmas, and truly celebrating the incarnation of the Lord, are not doing what the anti-Christmas crowd suggests. First, those in favor of the celebration do not add Christmas to the law or its interpretation of the law. Second, they do not say there is a purity in observing the day. Third, they do not undermine the law of God since there is no prohibition against esteeming a particular day or creating a celebration around a work of God. As opposed to the arguments put forth by those who are anti-Christmas, Christmas was formed from a love of God and to celebrate his miraculous work in history.

CELEBRATION

*P*erhaps it would be best to begin by defining "celebration." According to most dictionaries, a celebration is simply doing something special or enjoyable for a particular event, occasion, or holiday. It typically involves gathering with others with the same purpose in mind. Celebration is ultimately an act of thanksgiving, commemoration of an event, or a display of admiration of someone or their accomplishments. Celebration is not only a natural expression of humanity, but the Christian life is one of celebration, specifically of the character and work of the triune God and the Gospel.

To count every instance of rejoicing, praises, and celebrations in the Bible would be a long and arduous task. This is because from Genesis to Revelation, celebrations regarding who God is and what he has done ripple throughout the text. Sometimes a patriarch of the Old Testament would build an altar to God because of the goodness of God without an explicit command,[1] or the Israelites would rejoice because of God's care in the midst of their surrounding enemies. We celebrate many things, whether it be a job promotion, someone meeting the Lord, a baptism, the birth of someone in our lives, or an answered prayer. Celebrations are a normal part of the human experience, and as Christians we direct our thanksgiving to God due to a biblical worldview. With this simple reality in mind, it should be a given that celebrating the incarnation of Christ would be acceptable, but I want to demonstrate it regardless.

Joy and thanksgiving are key elements of celebration, and there are many examples of such celebrations in the Bible. Two examples can be found in the joy of Israelites at the completion of the temple featured in Ezra 3:10-13 and another in Nehemiah 12:27-43. Looking at Nehemiah, the text in verse 27 states,

> "And at the dedication of the wall of Jerusalem they sought the Levites in all their places, to bring them to Jerusalem to celebrate the dedication with gladness, with thanksgivings and with singing, with cymbals, harps, and lyres."

Within this text, we discover the nation of Israel finding the Levites and gathering with them to celebrate God's faithfulness in the completion of the wall by dedicating the wall to God. They planned a celebration and invited many in joy. They did so with songs, even assigning "two large choirs to give thanks," (v. 31), worship, and sacrifices. They celebrated God, his work, and his faithfulness, without a command to do so.

It is at this point that I am inclined to raise these simple questions: if Israel can celebrate the faithfulness of God in the rebuilding of the wall, then why can't Christians celebrate the faithfulness of God in the incarnation of Christ? Why should Christians be forbidden from marking, planning, and celebrating the culmination of God's promises being realized in Christ's coming to earth? Surely the coming of the high priest, prophet, and king, God the Son incarnate, anticipated for centuries, is worthy of celebration just as much as the rebuilding of the wall. I would suggest that we *all* know that such is worthy of celebration. We celebrate this truth constantly when we recall the Gospel, because without the incarnation of Christ, there would be no Gospel. With such an obvious statement, the debate actually becomes less about the ability as Christians to celebrate the coming of Christ and more about whether Christians can have an *annual* celebration, wherein we re-focus ourselves and reflect upon this glorious work on a reoccurring basis. Surely, we can according to the functions and purposes of festivals in the Old Testament, the traditions of Jews with Hanukkah, Paul's writings about days and seasons in Romans 14, and the celebrations of the incarnation in the New Testament. With all this said, I will happily say that Christmas *is a tradition*, and one that is non-binding on individuals. I will join the apostle Paul as he says, let each be fully convinced in his own mind.

A DETOUR

It is worth pointing out that many times Christmas is mistaken, even in Christian circles, to merely be the "birthday" of Jesus. The feast of the Nativity of Jesus is more than that because of the fundamental nature of Jesus himself. Yes, we celebrate the birth of Christ, but the tradition is more focused upon the birth of the incarnate Son. It is a celebration of the incarnation and the coming of the Gospel. To be reductionistic and claim it is merely the celebration of a birthday, as if Christ were not God the Son incarnate, is missing the point. We must also recognize that there *are* elements of tradition forged through time and culture within our contemporary setting that are unnecessary extras. Some of these do indeed tend to distract from the celebration of Christmas. To that point, each family needs to have those conversations if they desire to celebrate Christmas. This detour is not to discuss those details, but simply state the heart of the matter and central focus is the incarnation of Christ.

THE INCARNATION IN THE GOSPELS

*W*ithin the Gospel of Luke, we find much anticipation for the coming of Christ in the realization of Mary's pregnancy. The birth narrative begins in chapter 2 of Luke's Gospel when Mary and Joseph travel to Bethlehem for the census and Mary gives birth to Jesus. Verses 8-14 mention the following: the shepherds in the field (v. 8), the appearance of an angel (v. 9), the proclamation of the good news (v. 10), the message confirmed by the birth of Christ (v. 11-12), and the heavenly angels praising God at this event (v. 13-14). The angel speaking to the shepherds declares, "I bring you good news of great joy that will be for all the people, for unto you is born this day, in the city of David, a savior who is Christ the Lord." (v. 10-11)[1] The news brought to the shepherds is not only for them, but "will be for all people." Thompson comments, "Notes of joy resound throughout the infancy narratives and frame Luke's

Gospel," pointing to 1:14; 28; 44; 47; 58; 2:10; 24:52.[2] It is important to note the phrase, "news of great joy" and its connection to verse 11 "for unto you is born this day." Here the conjunction (ὅτι; translated as "for") is epexegetical, which means it explains "the content of the good news and reason for great joy."[3] Marshall continues, "a birth has taken place which will benefit the shepherds and all who hear the news."[4]

The good news first proclaimed to the shepherds is the birth of their long-awaited redeemer, and such news would bring joy for all people. Verse 12 confirms this by stating the baby can be seen wrapped in swaddling cloths and lying in a manger. In verse 13, we read that a multitude of angels (heavenly host) appear suddenly and in verse 14 they praise God. Marshall comments, "the angelic song is in effect a proclamation of the results of the birth of Jesus rather than a hymn of praise directly addressed to God."[5] Here we find worship and celebration elicited due to the birth of Jesus the Christ by angels, first and foremost. The good news and joy for all people is wrapped in swaddling cloths - God the Son incarnate, who will bring peace through reconciliation with God.

Following this event, the shepherds decide to go to Bethlehem to see what was proclaimed to them (v. 15), and exchange words with Mary and presumably Joseph. From there we read, "And the shepherds returned, while glorifying and praising God for all they had heard and seen, just as it was told to them."[6] Just as the numerous angels glorified and praised God over the birth of the Lord, so the shepherds follow suit. Surely the angelic host and men spontaneously worshipping God because of his miraculous work, was not abominable or sinful. The celebration and joy over the birth of this savior was not unfounded given the promise of redemption proclaimed for centuries prior.

From the protoevangelium with Adam and Eve, to the prophets, to the heavy messianic expectations during the intertestamental period, and through the conquest of Rome, the birth of the savior was worth celebrating after centuries of waiting. The shepherds, in their celebration of the birth of Jesus, didn't have access to all of the revelation we have now regarding the incarnate Son. They were not familiar with the prologue of the Gospel of John that marvels at the eternal Son taking on flesh, nor Paul's writings regarding the incarnation. Instead, they celebrated the birth of a messiah and praised God for his sending of this savior.

Though less focused upon the physical birth of Jesus, John's Gospel focuses its prologue on the pre-existent Christ and the incarnation of Jesus. The birth of Christ - the realization of the eternal Son of God taking on a human nature - is not only a miracle beyond others, but the beginning of the coming kingdom. It is the fulfillment of the law, the reconciliation of sinners, and a pivotal shift in the history of redemption. Types and shadows will reveal their substance as Jesus takes on flesh, and Gentiles will be brought in under the wing of the one true God. The incarnation is of such importance that John calls anyone who denies that Jesus took on flesh an antichrist (1 John 4:2). Stephen Wellum notes,

"Without the eternal Son's fully human birth, growth, and development, we would not have an all sufficient Savior whose sacrificial death achieved for us the full forgiveness of our sins and whose sympathetic service helps us to walk in the power of forgiveness."[7]

The incarnation is a miraculous and necessary event. It demonstrates the profound humility of the Son and demonstrates the coming of the long-awaited King. Just as Mary, Joseph (presumably), Elizabeth, John the Baptist in the womb, the multitude of angels, and shepherds celebrated the conception and birth of the savior and worshiped God, I find celebration of the incarnation to be a rich historical tradition that Christians can follow.

Continuing in our discussion, the tradition of giving gifts is often linked to the gifts presented to Jesus by the Magi, or "wise men," in the second chapter of Matthew. Nativity scenes will often present the shepherds, angels, and Magi all being united around the cradle of the infant Jesus. However, it is typically understood that Jesus was likely a toddler around the time the Magi visited. Early Nativity scenes tended to summarize events surrounding the birth narratives and so this simplified depiction came into play. Regardless, within this scene, we simply see the Magi come bearing gifts and worshiping Jesus (2:11). The foreign Magi, who are thought to have been Persians or Persian Jews, worship Jesus and this is in stark contrast to Herod. Herod, the imposed King of the Jews under the thumb of the Roman Empire, sought to kill dissenters and rid himself of any competition as the king of the

Jews. Chromatius, a 5th century church leader, puts the scene in vivid language in his tract on Matthew,

"Let us now observe how glorious was the dignity that attended the King after his birth, after the magi in their journey remained obedient to the star. For immediately the magi fell to their knees and adored the one born as Lord. There in his very cradle they venerated him with offerings of gifts, though Jesus was merely a whimpering infant. They perceived one thing with the eyes of their bodies but another with the eyes of the mind. The lowliness of the body he assumed was discerned, but the glory of his divinity is now made manifest. A boy he is, but it is God who is adored. How inexpressible is the mystery of his divine honor! The invisible and eternal nature did not hesitate to take on the weaknesses of the flesh on our behalf. The Son of God, who is God of the universe, is born a human being in the flesh. He permits himself to be placed in a manger, and the heavens are within the manger. He is kept in a cradle, a cradle that the world cannot hold. He is heard in the voice of a crying infant. This is the same one for whose voice the whole world would tremble in the hour of his passion. Thus he is the One, the God of glory and the Lord of majesty, whom as a tiny infant the magi recognize. It is he who while a child was truly God and King eternal. To him Isaiah pointed, saying, "For a boy has been born to you; a son has been given to you, a son whose empire has been forged on his shoulders."[8]

Adoration, desire to give gifts, and joyful worship filled the Magi's hearts. In addition to the birth narratives, there are many other texts to be observed within the Gospels that emphasize the sending of the Son, such as John 3:16. The magnificent work of the Father in sending the Son into the world is a profound reality that radically impacts human history.

THE INCARNATION IN THE LETTERS OF PAUL

*T*he incarnation is no small matter to Paul, and while again Christians can all agree on the magnificence of the incarnation, my argument goes a step further in suggesting that it is worthy of and permissible to hold a celebration in remembrance.[1] The first Pauline text to be highlighted is Galatians 4:1-7. The context of Galatians centers upon Paul rebuking a false teaching which taught that to attain salvation you must observe the law. The results of these teachings was that the law was being added to Christ and his work in order for one to gain salvation. This particular passage in Galatians 4:1-7 is extremely rich, but my examination of the text will be limited. The passage mentions God sending his Son to redeem those who are born under the law, whom Paul refers to as those "enslaved to the elementary principles of the world" in verse 3. Some commentators will note that "elementary principles" can also be applicable to Gentiles' basic concepts of morality rather than being limited to only the law given to the Jews. Paul notes that,

> "But when the fullness of time had come, God sent forth his son, born of a woman, born under the law, in order to redeem those under the law, so that we may receive adoption as sons. And because you are sons, God has sent the Spirit of his son into our hearts, calling out, "Abba, Father!" Thus, you are no longer a slave, but a son, and if a son, then also an heir through God" (Gal. 4:1-7).[2]

This text highlights the importance and impact of the incarnation with some observations. The first phrase of significance is, "the fullness of time." Paul states that this was a precise moment in human history wherein God sent Jesus into the world by his providence and wisdom. Discussions abound on the circumstances in which Jesus was born, lived, died, and was resurrected. I highly recommend one to read further on the historical circumstances of "the fullness of time," but the point I would like to make here is that God's means of redemption is revealed in a particular moment in history, beginning with the incarnation. The incarnation is not the end by any means, but rather a pivotal point in history theologically and providentially. Paul in Galatians moves on to state that God sent forth his Son, born of a woman. F.F. Bruce notes here that, "God's sending his Son coincides with his birth from a woman"[3] and this linked with Paul's expression, "the fullness of time," emphasizes the birth of the incarnate Son as being that first step in the great gift of redemption to humanity. On this subject, Bruce notes,

"But what is emphasized here is that the nodal point of salvation-history, marked by the coming of Christ (cf. 3:24, εἰς Χριστόν) or the coming of 'faith' (cf. 3:23, 25), constitutes the divinely ordained epoch for the people of God to enter into their inheritance as his mature and responsible sons and daughters. It is the coming of Christ that makes this particular epoch the πλήρωμα τοῦ χρόνου. Here it is the 'realized' aspect of Christian eschatology that Paul presents, the 'already' rather than the 'not yet'. The Galatians must understand that the period of tutelage is past; their spiritual majority has arrived."[4]

Of course, verse 5 cannot be disconnected from the passage, which emphasizes the work of Christ beyond his initial coming. This is to say, we recognize the work of Christ *in its entirety*, and so we must place things in their logical order when considering Jesus' work. Thus, the first logical work of Christ was his humility in taking on human flesh in humble obedience to the Father's will as noted in Phil. 2:5-11.

Paul's passage in Galatians further stresses that Jesus was born under the law to redeem those under the law so that they may receive adoption. Adoption is a glorious theological reality for the believer in Christ. For this to be gifted to individuals, it requires the work of the incarnation, and of Christ's being born of a woman under the law. This is so that we could receive the Holy Spirit, who proclaims in our hearts that God is our Father. The strong connection between the incarnation and adoption would eventually be stressed by many writers in the early church against errors related to Christ's human nature.[5] The incarnation is a work of Christ worth celebrating just as much as his death, burial, resurrection, and ascension. I would even postulate that we tend to forget that the incarnation is in fact a work of Christ in the triune God's plan of redemption.

From Galatians, we can examine one of my favorite texts on the incarnation, which is Philippians 2:5-11. Leading up to this target text, Paul has spoken about his current situation in Rome while calling the Philippians to live in a manner worthy of Christ. Paul calls those in Philippi to live in unity (1:27; 2:2), and to live contrary to those they encounter in Rome (1:16; 17). He instructs them to "Do nothing from selfish ambition or conceit, but in humility count others more significant than yourselves" (2:4). Additionally, Paul says that the Philippians should look to the interest of others (v. 4) and not merely the interests of oneself. In verse 5, Paul notes that this attitude should be that of the Philippians, as it was Christ's mind-set, "as expressed in the incarnation and crucifixion."[6] As the Philippians are told to put on this mind of Christ, what we learn about Jesus is that he did not look to his own interests, but to the interests of others (cf. 4). Not only this, but he counted others more significant than himself in humility (cf. 4). Paul moves on from verse 5 by providing an illustration for this assertion beginning in verse 6. The text reads,

"Have this mind among you, which was also Christ Jesus', who though, he existed in the form [dyn.[7] clothed in the glory] of God, did not consider equality with God as something to be exploited [dyn. to his own advantage] but emptied himself [dyn. stripped himself of his glory] by taking the form of a slave, having been born in the likeness of men. And found living as a man, he humiliated himself by becoming obedient to the point of death, even death on a cross."[8]

Paul expresses that Christ was in the form of God by utilizing the term μορφή (morphē). The term is often debated in regards to whether or not the term denotes ontological realties, but the term should be simply understood as "outward appearance."[9] Yet, while μορφή speaks to outward appearance, it does so in a way where the outward form of the subject is a genuine expression of that which underlines the subject,[10] thus, "Paul uses morphē to explain that Jesus truly and fully expresses the essence of God (v. 6) and the essence of a servant (v. 7)."[11] Further, the text in verse 6 pictures the preincarnate Son, donning the appropriate garments of glory and majesty in accordance with his social status. Not only is Christ described as being in the form of his splendor, glory, and status, but Paul expresses that Christ is equal with God. Hellerman notes that such language, "equality with [a] God," was common in ancient writers who wished to demonstrate power and status along with "godlike position of influence and prestige in the cosmos."[12]

Furthermore, the remarkable preincarnate Son is not only described as being equal to God, but he does not see his power and status as something to be used for his own advantage. The passage assumes the deity of Christ, and Paul is stressing that Jesus did not take such equality with God and exploit it for his own gain. Fee expresses this further by stating that this was contrary to the gods and lords which permeated the world of the Philippians.[13]Rather than exploiting his power and status, God the Son "emptied himself" by adding to himself a human nature for the sake of others.

As with μορφή, many debates surround the term κενόω or the "emptying" of Christ. Many commentators have properly pointed out that this term denotes an emptying, or putting away, of prestige or privilege.[14] Paul's elaboration of the phrase, "emptied himself," highlights this by stating that Christ took upon himself the μορφή of a slave. Such emptying is the humbling of the Son, not ontologically, but rather by addition of a lowly status and obedience unto death.[15] While many would opt for the less offensive term "servant" here in Philippians, it would be best to retain the term "slave" in translation. This is the only instance where the term δοῦλος (slave) is used for Christ making it particularly noteworthy, but also relevant to the context. Additionally, the term itself in juxtaposition to the μορφή of Christ prior to "emptying himself," would have been jarring for the Philippians.

Considering the social pecking order of the Roman Empire and placing slaves within it properly, we can understand why "the notion of a Being of equal rank to God willingly 'taking on the form of a slave' would have struck residents of Roman Philippi as abject folly."[16] Such folly can be understood by recognizing that slaves were at the bottom of the social order, especially because they were, by law, inferior and categorically separate from the individuals who lived in freedom. The important qualification is that Christ did not become a slave in a literal sense, but rather "in a relative sense – relative, that is, to his preincarnate status."[17] As it is stated by Oakes, the long drop from the status of God to the status of a human being was so significant that it was like taking on the form of a slave.[18] This taking on the form of a slave is expressed in verses 7 and 8 by noting that Jesus became a man. Silva points out that the terms, "slave" and "man" do not need to be pressed to find theological differences, but rather that the former notes the servitude of Jesus and "the latter simply reminds us that he gave expression to that attitude by becoming a man."[19]

In Philippians, then, we are faced with Jesus Christ, the kind and compassionate King and Savior. He is the eternal Son of God, who put away that which he could have exploited in order to humiliate himself in obedience to the Father for the sake of bringing a people into the kingdom of Heaven.

CONCLUSION

*P*erhaps we should conclude this discussion with the sentiments of some of the faithful saints who came before us. We can begin by looking at Charles Spurgeon, who is often noted as despising and opposing Christmas. Spurgeon has often been quoted in attempts to rebuke me for my views of Christmas, however many do not realize Spurgeon had a complicated relationship with Christmas. He spoke of his disapproval for the day because of the abuses of it leading to gluttony and drunkenness, and he is quoted as disliking the date of December 25th. I agree with his first point, and am not yet entirely convinced of December 25th being a realistic dating of the Nativity, but rather a traditional placeholder.

What often gets overlooked by the anti-Christmas crowd who quote Spurgeon's disapproval of the holiday is that Spurgeon also loved Christmas and sometimes spoke fondly of it. At one point, he even preaching twelve sermons on the day saying, "I wish there were twenty Christmas days in the year."[1] Spurgeon is further documented as participating in the festivities of Christmas, even dressing as Santa Clause to deliver gifts to orphans.[2] The Spurgeon Center further points out that Spurgeon valued the day because of the importance placed upon family, and that he "leveraged the holiday for the Gospel. He saw Christmas as an opportunity to tell an old story about the "the grandest light in history"[3]

Moving further back in time, we find the reformers of the 16th century differed from each other in their undertaking of Christmas. John Calvin in particular,

"sought to reclaim Christmas as a celebration of Christ's Nativity, a defining moment for Christians, without making the festival binding on the faithful. At the same time, his intention was to purge the holiday of the excesses of public exuberance traditionally associated with both the feast and what he viewed as the 'abomination' of the Mass."[4]

As you can see, John Calvin had similar issues as Spurgeon did with the abuse of the day. Bruce continues,

"For the Frenchman, Christmas and Easter formed the two most holy days of the year, and he set aside his regular practice of preaching through the books of the Bible, known as lectio continua, to hold sermons on the Nativity and the Passion of Christ. Some of Calvin's most moving words from the pulpit flowed from his preaching at Christmas. Speaking on the Nativity of Christ, Calvin drew his audience to consider the transformative joy of festival, declaring that it was a time for celebration in this world in preparation for the next."[5]

Calvin's letters on the subject would be shared by colleague Heinrich Bullinger. In his work "the Second Helvetic Confession" Bullinger noted,

"Moreover, if the churches do religiously celebrate the memory of the Lord's Nativity, Circumcision, Passion, Resurrection, and of his Ascension into heaven, and the sending of the Holy Spirit upon his disciples, according to Christian liberty, we do very well approve of it. But as for festival days, ordained for men or saints departed, we cannot allow of them."

Stepping back in time further, I wish to quote one more church figure, solely in regards to his exposition on the incarnation and its importance. Before the council of Nicaea and the Arian controversy, a church writer named Irenaeus lived between AD 130-200. He is considered one of the greatest Christian theologians of the early church, and penned the work, "Against Heresies," which combatted a movement rooted in Gnosticism. Within this work, Irenaeus speaks to the importance and necessity of the incarnation, stating,

"For it was for this end that the Word of God was made man, and He who was the Son of God became the Son of man, that man, having been taken into the Word, and receiving the adoption, might become the son of God. For by no other means could we have attained to incorruptibility and immortality, unless we had been united to incorruptibility and immortality. But how could we be joined to incorruptibility and immortality, unless, first, incorruptibility and immortality had become that which we also are, so that the corruptible might be swallowed up by the incorruptibility, and the mortal by immortality, that might receive the adoption of sons?"[6]

While there are many other faithful saints of the past who could be spoken of, such as Athanasius who penned the work, "On the Incarnation," I will conclude. While an individual is not bound or obligated to celebrate the incarnation, there are grounds to justify this celebration. As previously mentioned, there *are some* elements of tradition that can distract from the celebration of Christmas. However, such distractions and abuses do not negate the reality that the incarnation is worth celebrating. Each family should have those conversations if they desire to celebrate Christmas. While I have put forward my thoughts and considerations on the subject, let each of us, as Paul says, be convinced in our own mind and glorify God in whatever conviction we hold. Love the brethren regardless of their convictions on this subject, and thank God for redeeming love expressed in the Father sending his Jesus Christ on our behalf.

"Christ is born, glorify Him! Christ from heaven, go out to meet Him! Christ on earth, be exalted! Sing to the Lord all the whole earth; and that I may join both in one word, let the heavens rejoice, and let the earth be glad, for Him who is of heaven and then of earth. Christ in the flesh, rejoice with trembling and with joy; with trembling because of your sins, with joy because of your hope."

  - Gregory Nazianzen (4th century)

"This day He Who Is, is born; and He Who Is becomes what He was not"

  – John Chrysostom (4th century)

PART IV
EASTER AND PAGANISM

INTRODUCTION

$\mathcal{A}$s we move into the topic of Easter and Paganism, you will discover a lot of the same principles that have been discussed with Christmas. With those in mind, you will find that Easter is much easier to deal with in terms of its history. The primary debate surrounds the term "Easter" itself, and so the linguistics will be a topic of discussion. Once that problem is resolved, most of the discussion flows seamlessly. Some of the same presuppositions mentioned in part two also apply here, such as the reality that the world will act as we would expect, and will try to secularize anything. Additionally, the church will sometimes adopt the culture to appeal to the culture. However, regardless of how the secular world attempts to secularize the holiday, everyone is still talking about Jesus whether negatively or positively. Even when critiquing Easter and trying to change its purpose and meaning, individuals are still speaking of Jesus.

After much investigation, I've found that many of the myths regarding Easter are linked to none other than Alexander Hislop, whom we discussed in Part 2: Christmas and Paganism. To summarize that discussion, Hislop essentially single handedly began the unsubstantiated assertions that the Babylonian cult of Nimrod was celebrated by Rome, and reformers needed to purge Christianity of those "pagan" holidays. This was knee jerk reaction to Catholicism. According to Hislop in his work "The Two Babylons," he claims that Satan allowed Constantine to take over the true faith and led it to idol worship. Hislop followed along with the same line of reasoning on Easter, and concluded that it was worship of an ancient pagan deity. As we proceed, we will interact with a popular image often circulated online that was created by an atheist who seems to utilize some of Hislop's arguments.

Like with Christmas, I am operating with certain theological and worldview presuppositions that are worth noting, and can be ascertained in part two. They are just as applicable with Easter as they are with Christmas, and as Christians, I believe they are worth keeping in mind. We will move onto the claims against Easter and the negative case.

CHEAP PAGANISM

Our first point of interest deals with various assumptions that come into play when discussing these topics. If these are not addressed, we will ultimately find conversations going in endless circles, more so than they already do. The first and most basic question worth addressing is what exactly is paganism, and what constitutes a pagan practice? Why does this need to be addressed? Within these discussions, we often do not understand what paganism is and what makes something pagan. In truth, I have found that many times, 'pagan' is used as a catchall for things a particular individual does not like. Furthermore, something is often deemed pagan merely because it correlates with natural phenomena, such as the elements found in various seasons.

This is not the case for everyone using this label for Easter, as many genuinely believe Easter can be linked back to Ishtar or Eostre. Still, for others, when pressed on the historical data of the Ishtar and Eostre claims, they will resort to, 'well, it is still pagan,'[1] many times with the assumption that because it is not found explicitly commanded in the Bible, it must be pagan.

I suppose this is true to the extent that before Christianity, we were all pagans, and pagans used everything, but what about those things that were formed by Christians for Christian purposes, for Christian realities? For many, even those things are pagan because they are not explicitly found in the Bible and are to be rejected. Nonetheless, we should question the conception of 'paganism' being presented to others because the claim of 'paganism' is thrown around flippantly. What makes something 'pagan', and what is paganism?

Paganism comes from the Latin term paganus, which originally referred to something akin to 'rustic.' In its religious meaning, it is a term that describes the 'pagan,' the one who belongs to ancient polytheism. While the specifics about the origins of the religious meaning are debated, it is clear that it was only in the 4th century that writers used paganus in the sense that many Christians use it today. The first document, dated roughly between AD 300-330, is an inscription that describes a girl who was born as a pagan but was baptized. Before this term's usage, Christians would often separate themselves as unique amongst the "Greeks" and the "Jews," sometimes utilizing the word for "nations."

Where agreement is found in scholarship is that the terms "pagan" and "paganism" took hold and were moved into a religious meaning and utilized to describe those who believed in false gods and performed for them rituals, practices, customs, etc.[2] In essence, because Christians utilized it in the 4th century, the term came to denote non-Christian polytheism. This becomes ironic when Christians are trying to claim that Easter is pagan as it was the Christians who both observed Easter historically and gave these modern Christians that usage of 'pagan' they want to label Easter with. Further, this understanding of paganism arose at a time when many Christians erroneously believe all of Christendom was corrupted via Nicaea and Constantine, a myth that plagues modern Evangelicals and betrays a lack of church history.

All of this, however, shows that 'paganism' is a broad term, especially within the era of Neo-paganism that we live in today. Paganism overall reaches around the globe with various histories, practices, and even appropriations of other groups. Paganism utilizes nearly anything and everything in the natural world to honor a deity or deities. It has a variety of practices that are too broad to focus on here. Still, the point should be pretty clear: paganism denotes the dedication to a deity, and pagan practices, rituals, etc. are concentrated toward the deity you have adopted. It is a conscious and intentional worship of a pagan god. Further complicating matters is the reality that pagans have utilized everything ranging from wood to water to fire, for their pagan symbols. Still, these symbols are not owned by pagans and only become pagan when there is a worship of a deity involved.

Christians will hardly stop using fire, water, and wood because pagans used them, but they will refuse to go near eggs and rabbits? Toothbrushes and toilet paper, though being 'pagan' at their inception and origin, do not evoke a deity when used in our day-to-day lives, and I have yet to meet a Christian who has abandoned these items because of their pagan origins. This principle will come into play later but can be summarized as follows: pagans cannot claim God's creation, creatures, etc., as their own. If we gave pagans everything they have utilized for their idolatry, we would have little left. Nonetheless, for now, it is sufficient to say if something is not being used to worship a pagan deity, then it is not pagan.

Some Objects and Animals used by Pagans:

- Stones
- Crystals
- Plants
- Herbs
- Trees
- Feathers
- Shells
- Antlers
- Claws
- Deer and antelopes
- Wolves and dogs
- Cats
- Birds
- Snakes

- Bees
- Foxes
- Fish
- Dragons

Some Item usages and Symbols:

- Salt used for purification or protection
- Water for washing rituals, purification
- Leaves for rituals related to changing seasons
- Wood for altars, ritual tools, idols
- Oils for anointing
- Candles for worship, altars
- Cats, dogs, birds as spirit guides
- Chalices/cups for rituals
- Mirrors for scrying and divination
- Bells for purification, ritual music, calling spirits
- Horses as symbols of strength and freedom
- Bees as symbols of community
- Butterflies as symbols of rebirth, transformation
- Beavers as symbols of hard work
- Otters as symbols of joy, community
- Wolves as symbols of loyalty, strength
- Rings symbols for unbroken commitments
- Trees as symbol of life, growth, wisdom
- Fire as a symbol of transformation, purification, illumination

- Water as a symbol of the flow of life, purification, renewal
- The earth as a symbol of stability, grounding
- Wind as a symbol of change, movement, communication
- Sky as a symbol of vastness, mystery, divine inspiration
- Mountains as symbols of strength, endurance, and spiritual growth
- Colors had various symbolic meanings
- Natural phenomena in seasons had symbols

Some Deities and Symbols Used for Them:

- ODIN [NORSE] Ravens, Wolves
- PERSEPHONE [GREEK] Poppy Flowers, Sheep, Pomegranates
- DEMETER [GREEK] Wheat and grains, Poppy Flowers, Deer
- BRIZO [GREEK] Anchors, Nets, Fish/Dolphins
- FREYR [NORSE] Boar, Ship, Wheat
- HECATE [GREEK] Keys, Crossroads, Dogs
- CERNUNNOS [CELTIC] Antlers, Trees - Oak in Particular, Stags
- LUGH [CELTIC] Weapons, Musical Instruments, Oak Trees

What further complicates all of these discussions is the reality that pagans, because of their agricultural roots, had major events based on seasons, lunar calendars, solar calendars, and so forth. This was the case within the era of the Israelites in the Ancient Near East, as those peoples "observed many special sacred occasions at various times of the year, such as beginnings of months, one or both of the equinoxes, and seasons tied to the agricultural cycle."[3] This has led many to conclude that Easter must be pagan because it falls in the Spring and can be correlated with pagan Spring Festivals.[4] Yet, why does this complicate the current discussion? Simply because,

"Israelite festivals were similar to other ancient Near Eastern festivals in that they revolved around the agricultural cycle, celebrated the sovereignty and beneficence of the deity and harvests that he provided, included special festival offerings, provided for renewal of the cult by purification of the sanctuary and in several cases involved feasting by the people. However, the Israelite festivals were simpler than many other ancient Near Eastern festivals, and some Israelite sacred occasions were unique in that they explicitly commemorated the historical deliverance of the nation by their deity."[5]

The issue should be obvious, and things are further complicated in the reality that humans rarely have original thoughts, and themes around seasons find parallels globally because of the agricultural focus and the predictability of seasons. This means that there are overlaps in observations in nature and themes in particular seasons and in the festivals that fall within those seasons. Why are certain living greenery symbols of life in the Winter? Because everything else has died! Why does Spring have so many symbols of New Life? Because agriculturally, things were 'springing' to life. These aren't profound thoughts but observations of God's created order. The fact that a season, such as spring, is associated with 'new life,' restoration, and baby animals doesn't make it inherently pagan; it just demonstrates the predictability of the human mind as it observes God's created world. This point is usually dismissed, so we can use Passover as an example because, as we will see later, Easter is closely connected to Passover. Myjewishlearning.com begins its explanation of Passover and the Spring with the following,

> "The Torah places great stress on the fact that Passover occurs in the spring. In biblical times, the month in which the holiday fell was called Aviv (spring). During the first exile in Babylon, the months were given Babylonian names. Passover's month was renamed Nisan. Although the name shifted, the Hebrews upheld the Torah's insistence on the link of spring and Passover... Biblical language and symbol point to spring as the proper season for deliverance. The rebirth of earth after winter is nature's indication that life overcomes death: spring is nature's analogue to redemption. Life blossoming, breaking winter's death grip, gives great credence to the human yearning for liberation."[6]

Aside from this paragraph being similar to how Christians would speak of the resurrection around Easter, this type of language is present in various literature, ancient and modern - pagan, Jewish, and Christian. The reason is simple: we are not blind, deaf, or dumb to the seasons God has put in place, and such themes will resonate across the world because of God's general or natural revelation. Ancient Jews using similar spring themes as pagans around them made Passover no more pagan than Easter is for having similar themes. I would argue that modern Christians have lost some of these natural observances and the parallels that ancient Christians would draw between the events of the Bible and nature.

Yet, we are getting ahead of ourselves as we simply need to point out that for something to be pagan - that is dedicated to a polytheistic deity - they need to be dedicated to a polytheistic deity. An altar used between various temples and churches means nothing without that altar being used to worship a particular deity. The altar is not inherently pagan, no more than Abraham's various altars were inherently Canaanite. What made it an altar to pagan deities, pagan, was its dedication to said deity, usually enclosed in a temple for said deity and unmistakably designed for that deity. To this, I'd say if one is going to call something pagan, they must be able to do the following: 1) abide by a meaningful definition of paganism, 2) identify the deity being worshiped, 3) demonstrate that said deity is actually being worshiped via the items, practices, etc involved.

LINGUISTICS AND EASTER

With the preliminary out of the way regarding what constitutes paganism and pagan practice, we can nip one of the most significant issues in the bud. It would be dishonest to say this was an easy issue, but it would be equally disingenuous to load it with conspiracy. What problem are we discussing? The term "Easter" itself and where it comes from.

While some move to erroneously connect the term 'Easter' with the ancient goddess 'Ishtar,' to be discussed below, a more meaningful discussion is on the connection between Easter and a goddess that may have existed named Eostre. What often isn't expressed, however, is that there is more debate on the subject than the certainty of the internet allows for. There is much debate on the topic, with the two positions by scholars being a) there is no connection given a lack of evidence and b) there is a possible connection yet challenging to prove because of the evidence. This means that the certainty individuals posit on the subject is, at best, a possibility, but it is doubtful and difficult to prove.

Our earliest known reference to Eostre comes from the 8th-century monk Bede, who wrote that the month of April was called Eosturmonath in Old English in honor of the goddess Eostre. Thus, some scholars believe that this is evidence that the Christian holiday of Easter has its roots in a pre-Christian pagan celebration of the spring equinox associated with Eostre. However, other scholars have pointed out that there is no evidence for a pre-Christian festival of Eostre and that Bede's reference is the only known mention of her. In his article "The Origin of the Name 'Easter': A Textual Perspective," J. Edward Walters argues that the connection between Easter and Eostre is tenuous at best and that Bede's reference to the goddess is the only evidence we have for her existence.[1] Walters, among others, suggests that the name "Easter" may derive from the Old High German word eostarun, which means "dawn," and was used to describe the rising of the sun on the spring equinox.[2] There are a lot of discussions about Bede and the reliability of his testimony, but what has been said thus far stands – the connection is, at best, a doubtful and difficult-to-prove possibility.

A more accessible discussion on the subject is found at Answers in Genesis in the article, "Is the Name Easter of Pagan Origin?" The article helpfully begins by introducing readers to individuals who would heavily propagate various claims of pagan syncretism, namely with the intention of polemics against the Roman Catholic Church.[3] In his original book Babylon Mystery Religion, one of the individuals, Ralph Woodrow, claimed that Eostre is connected to Easter. Yet, Woodrow shifted his position and updated his work, "The Babylon Connection?" In his updated book, he now demonstrates the false conclusions and methodology of Alexander Hislop.

While Woodrow once utilized Hislop's work and supported it, he now does not, but it is the first edition of Woodrow's work that is often appealed to. This said, Hislop is ultimately where the connection between Eostre, Easter, and Ishtar comes from. Yet Hislop's reasoning is incomprehensible. His case largely rests upon the idea that the similarities between the *sounds* of the deity's names (Ishtary and Eostre) and Easter are enough to prove his claims. What do I mean by the sound of their names? In essence, because one word sounds the same as another, it must be derivative in some shape or form from the other. This logic becomes a wormhole of problems when considering the numerous terms that sound the same yet obviously have no connection. For example, what is stopping an individual from connecting the Biblical figure Esther to Ishtar, which has a closer resemblance than Ishtar does to Easter?[4]

As the article by Patterson moves into the discussion on Bede and the connection to Eostre, Patterson explains that the English and German terms may have been developed independently of this goddess or could be related to her in some shape or form. Others will argue that

"Easter" has its root in the German word for resurrection; Nick Sayers states the following,

> "Because the English Anglo/Saxon language originally derived from the Germanic, there are many similarities between German and English. Many English writers have referred to the German language as the "Mother Tongue!" The English word Easter is of German/Saxon origin and not Babylonian as Alexander Hislop falsely claimed. The German equivalent is Oster. Oster (Ostern being the modern-day equivalent) is related to Ost which means the rising of the sun, or simply in English, east. Oster comes from the old Teutonic form of auferstehen / auferstehung, which means resurrection, which in the older Teutonic form comes from two words, Ester meaning first, and stehen meaning to stand. These two words combine to form erstehen which is an old German form of auferstehen, the modern day German word for resurrection."[5]

As Patterson explains,

> "In the Hebrew, Passover is Pesach. The Greek form is simply a transliteration and takes the form Pascha. Virtually all languages refer to Easter as either a transliterated form of pascha or use resurrection in the name. English and German stand apart in their use of Easter (Ostern) to refer to the celebration of the Resurrection."[6]

This is seen reflected in early German and English translations of the Bible. John Wycliffe translated the New Testament in English in 1382 from the Latin Vulgate and merely transliterated the word Pascha to Pask rather than translating it. Martin Luther, though, in his German New Testament, 1522, would choose the term Oster to refer to the Passover both in instances before and after the Resurrection.

For our purposes here, the most notable translation is the work of William Tyndale, who was the first to translate the Bible into English from Hebrew and Greek. In his New Testament, he uses the word ester (easter) to refer to the Passover. In Tyndale's translation, he would utilize the term 29 times in its New Testament occurrences. Yet when he came to the Old Testament translation, he coined a new word, Passover, and used it within the Old Testament. He likely realized that Easter in its English context (being connected to the resurrection) would be problematic or confusing within the pre-resurrection context of the Old Testament.

This humorously means two things: 1) Easter *predates* Passover *as an English term,* and 2) the individual who coined Passover for the English-speaking world was content using Easter in his translation of the New Testament. Following Tyndale's English Bible, Matthew's Bible of 1537 utilizes Passover in the Old Testament and Easter in its various chapter summaries. The Great Bible of 1539 also uses Passover in the Old Testament and Easter in fifteen New Testament Passages. Over time, translations would replace Easter with Passover, particularly in the Geneva Bible, the Bishop's Bible, and eventually the King James Bible. Still, for debated reasons, the King James retains "Easter" in Acts 12:4. Some argue it was theological, others accidental – but this is irrelevant to our particular focus. Patterson summarizes the discussion as follows,

"It would seem from the translations of Luther and Tyndale that by 1500, the word oster/ester simply referred to the time of the Passover feast and had no association with the pagan goddess Eostre. Even if the word had an origin in her name, the usage had changed to such a degree that Luther was comfortable referring to Christ as the Osterlamm. On the other hand, Cruse's Resurrection etymology is also consistent with this passage, and Luther referred to Christ as the "Resurrection lamb." Likewise, Tyndale was comfortable referring to Christ as the esterlambe.

To suggest these men thought of their Savior in terms of the sacrificial offering of a pagan goddess is quite absurd in light of their writings and translations of other portions of Scripture. Even the translators of the KJV, who relied heavily on Tyndale's work, chose to use Easter in the post-Resurrection context of Acts 12:4. Using a word that means resurrection would not make sense to describe the Passover festivals prior to the Resurrection of Christ. However, Luther still used oster consistently in his New Testament."[7]

In the same vein as these English translators of the Bible, Easter is used in many English translations of ancient Christian works and church histories. In his edition of Eusebius's History of the Church, Paul Maier notes that "the Greek Pascha-paschal festival or Passover is translated as Easter for the benefit of modern readers, a term used only later in church history."[8]

The scholars who compiled the three-volume Encyclopedia of Ancient Christianity utilize the term, as well as modern church Historian Nick Needham. The reason why is quite simple: until widespread propagation of the idea that Easter was a pagan word, Christians understood it as the celebration of the resurrection. While many who are skeptical of Easter will reject this and boil it down to wholesale corruption of the Christian church, I reject that assessment. I also have difficulty understanding how the term, if being pagan and inherently so, became a well-used translation of Pascha for the length of time it did. Even if the doubtful possibility that Easter is connected to Eostre is true, history has long forgotten Eostre (as we don't even know if she existed) in the same way that many who put on a product of Nike have no idea that Nike is a pagan deity.

To summarize, the term Easter became and remains a traditional and normative term for the commemoration of the resurrection. It helpfully differentiates between the Jewish Passover (that is, the Passover without regard to the resurrection and apart from the Christian tradition) and the Christian observance of the death, burial, and resurrection of Christ as our Pascha lamb. Easter was utilized because Pascha was celebrated in the spring, and Easter was an English term to denote the season or as Bede stated, the month. We have "Easter" as the traditional Old English name, a translation of Pascha, for the holiday commemorating the resurrection. When it comes to translating Pascha, Germanic languages are the oddballs, and in other languages, there are more resemblances to Pascha. In fact, within the Greek-speaking world, Easter is referred to as Pascha to this day while recognizing that Easter is an English translation of such.

From here, I will be referring to the commemoration of the resurrection, or resurrection day, as Easter. While Easter as a term was a development dependent upon the development of the English language, the celebration of the resurrection pre-dates Bede's account mentioned above by many years (see chapter 19). What I mean is this: even if you disagree with the 'name' or designation of Easter because you feel as if it is a Germanic Goddess, the celebration of the resurrection was occurring in the Ancient Christian World before the term Easter came to designate the celebration. One can call it Pascha if desired, but it is an ancient celebration.

THE NEGATIVE CASE

Whenever we look to the discussion on Easter and its alleged pagan roots, most of the controversy is indeed found in the term "Easter" itself. If you go to a site such as history.com and look up the history of Easter you'll read,

"Easter is a Christian holiday that celebrates the belief in the resurrection of Jesus Christ. In the New Testament of the Bible, the event is said to have occurred three days after Jesus was crucified by the Romans and died in roughly 30 AD The holiday concludes the "Passion of Christ," a series of events and holidays that begins with Lent—a 40-day period of fasting, prayer and sacrifice—and ends with Holy Week, which includes Holy Thursday (the celebration of Jesus' Last Supper with his 12 Apostles, also known as "Maundy Thursday"), Good Friday (on which Jesus' crucifixion is observed) and Easter Sunday. Although a holiday of high religious significance in the Christian faith, many traditions associated with Easter date back to pre-Christian, pagan times."[1]

Further down the page, under the heading, "Why is Easter called Easter" it reads,

"St. Bede the Venerable, the 6th century author of Historia ecclesiastica gentis Anglorum ("Ecclesiastical History of the English People"), maintains that the English word "Easter" comes from Eostre, or Eostrae, the Anglo Saxon goddess of spring and fertility. Other historians maintain that "Easter" derives from in albis, a Latin phrase that's plural for alba, or "dawn," that became eostarum in Old High German, a precursor to the English language of today. Despite its significance as a Christian holy day, many of the traditions and symbols that play a key role in Easter observances actually have roots in pagan celebrations—particularly the pagan goddess Eostre—and in the Jewish holiday of Passover."[2]

While the History Channel puts Bede in the 6th century, he lived during the late 7th and 8th century, with his "Ecclesiastical History of the English People" most likely being penned in the 8th century. It should be noted that the history channel cites the document and dates the document in the 8th century as well. This means there was a typo or mistake, but it was a significant one given that this is a two-century difference. Regardless, what Bede writes in "The Reckoning of Time" is,

> "Eosturmonath has a name which is now translated as 'Paschal month,' and which was once called after a goddess of theirs named Eostre, in whose honor feasts were celebrated in that month. Now they designate the Paschal season by her name, calling the joys of the new rite by the time-honoured name of the old observance" (De temporum ratione or "The Reckoning of Time")

The first claim made by Bede is that the term Eostre changed its fundamental meaning. While it was once the name of a goddess, it would later be translated as "paschal month" (or Passover month). This makes sense when you make the connection of Eostre/Spring and the Passover/Resurrection being in the Spring. What we could have here is a partial truth in regards to the usage of the word. However, the claim is extended in our day to say that because this term is used, there are 'pagan' roots of Easter. This claim becomes so extended that we begin to find some pretty wild assertions. The culprit of a major extension was made in 2013 via an image that you may have seen. The image has a depiction of Ishtar, a pagan goddess, and reads,

> "This is Ishtar: pronounced Easter. Easter was originally a celebration of Ishtar,

the Assyrian and Babylonian goddess of fertility and sex. Her symbols (like the egg and bunny) were and still are fertility and sex symbols (or did you actually think eggs and bunnies had anything to do with the resurrection?). After Constantine decided to Christianize the Empire, Easter was

changed to represent Jesus. But at its roots, Easter (which is how you pronounce Ishtar) is all about celebrating fertility and sex."

According to this image, Easter is a Babylonian goddess, and the pagan roots of Easter are evident. This leads those viewing the image to conclude that Christianity is just trying to assimilate pagan worship. The claim in this image then exploded into numerous other images about other deities such as Ostra and Isis! I want to point out that this meme is not only false but was created and propagated by an atheist on a Richard Dawkins Facebook page. It is likely that this atheist utilized the work of Hislop for the image, given some of the images' claims. As it has been mentioned before, refuting these types of claims ultimately amounts to asking for original sources to support them, because many of them are factually inaccurate.[3] You'll recall the same issue occurred in the Pseudo-gods section of the Christmas examination. An interesting point is that there are now many atheists who note that these claims are false[4] and exhorts atheists to stop using them since they're dishonest and ahistorical.

Despite this, I'd like to look closer at the specific claims being made in this image. First, Ishtar is not pronounced "Easter." It is written as Ishtar as a transliteration. That means that it is written how it would be pronounced, "Ish-tar." Maybe "EEsh-tar," which is closer to Easter, but not quite Easter. This is simple, but important, given so much of the rhetoric is emphatic on this claim. So much so that even a second parenthetical statement is needed! A problem with this argument is that according to Bede, "Easter/Ishtar" didn't become used until the 8th century, in England. If Easter is connected to an ancient Babylonian goddess, then why is the term adopted from an anglo-saxon goddess according to other historical sources? Somewhere along the line we must assume that Ishtar, a Babylonian goddess, became Eostre, an anglo-saxon goddess. From there, Eostre would be adopted in the 8th century as the word to be a translation for "Passover."

It is worth noting that the image links Easter to the 4th century with Constantine, but it doesn't explain how "Easter," a term adopted sometime around the 8th century in England, was utilized in the 4th century. The image also does not explain the connection to Ishtar. I would postulate that if this claim regarding Ishtar were true, "Easter" would have been seen at the forming of this Christian holiday, yet we don't find it used until much later than Constantine. Contrary to the claims of the image, most pagan gods weren't the god or goddess of such broad categories. Ishtar was a counter to a Sumerian goddess who became the goddess "Astarte." She was *loosely* linked to fertility, but was mostly known as the goddess of kingship and war, sexuality, and Venus. Ishtar was *never* associated with eggs and bunnies, but rather a star, dove, sphinx, lion, and a gate. In regards to Constantine, he decreed the legalization, or more accurately the toleration, of Christianity in 313 with the edict in Milan. He was predominately neutral in his reign and admittedly had some influence in favor of his new-found faith, but it was Theodosius who made Christianity the state religion in 380, not Constantine as the image implies. There was mention of Easter (the celebration, not the term) in AD 325 at Nicaea, but it wasn't forcing a pagan holiday on the world. What occurred at Nicaea will be discussed in the positive case.

As mentioned previously, the popular meme shared by skeptics and Christians alike is not only false but was created and propagated by an atheist on a Richard Dawkins Facebook page. Interestingly enough, the meme that began the domino effect, has been redacted by the Facebook page's parent page, the Center for Inquiry in 2021. The article headline, "Holy Ishtar! Our Own False Claim Rises from the Dead" and goes on to say, "here's the thing. It's not true."[5] To just quote the source on the point,

> "In the years that this meme has been circulating, several outlets have posted refutations, most recently the news service Agence France-Presse, which is how it

came to our attention. As the article points out, "Easter" is derived from an Old High German word, "eostarum," which simply means, well, the East, and also refers to the dawn. The piece also notes that there may be a connection to a different pagan goddess, Eostre, but apparently that is mostly speculative. And as for Ishtar? The holiday has nothing to do with her. And no, "Ishtar" is not pronounced like "Easter" either. At best, it might be pronounced "EEsh-tar," but they are simply not related words. Religious traditions evolve over time, and Easter almost certainly has roots that go back further than Christianity, with influences from older religious and secular traditions. So even if the Ishtar meme *was* true, it wouldn't make any of the supernatural claims associated with the holiday any more or less credible. It remains that there are no such things as gods or goddesses, Jesus of Nazareth never rose from the dead, and a magic bunny does not deliver eggs to children. But more to the point: We were wrong."[6]

As the article mentions, the claims have been refuted a number of times, in various capacities, and while the article doesn't address all of the claims in detail, we'll find the claim regarding Constantine debunked below. Some time spent in researching leads one to see both secular and Christian sources finding an agreement that Ishtar having connections to Easter lacks any meaningful evidence. Ultimately the claim hardly deserves attention, especially when even mocking atheists are content to concede [and argue] the point that there is no connection to be made. To this I simply say, if the backhanded article by atheists can admit there is no connection, I would hope that Christians could be honest and admit such as well.

The truth is that despite all of the internet's postured certainty, our knowledge of "Eostre" is from the singular source of Bede. In his work, quoted above, he states that April is named after Eostre. There's no other historical documentation of this figure. Some scholars, like Philipp Shaw in "Pagan Goddesses in the Early Germanic World," point out that there are place names that *could* refer to this goddess. Others have said that the middle English name of Estrild, from Eosturhild, could point to this being the name of the goddess. Others conclude that Bede was correct only in that Anglo-Saxons used the name for the *month*, not necessarily a goddess. The festivals he mentions become even more difficult to track historically. This is to say, there are many questions with few answers in regards to the term "Easter," despite the internet's bold claims.

THE POSITIVE CASE AND THE
CONTROVERSY OF EASTER

*a*s mentioned, I will be referring to the commemoration of the resurrection, Pascha, or resurrection day, as Easter. With Ishtar out of the way and the later claim of the goddess having its documentation in the 8th century, we can look a little more closely at Easter, its history, and controversy. When we look at volumes on church history, church historians agree that Easter is the most ancient Christian 'feast' or observation. The Church Historian Nick Needham, who takes a negative position on the roots of Christmas,[1] has this to say about Easter,

> "Christian worship revolved around Sunday, or the Lord's day" as the early Church called it – the day on which the Lord Jesus had risen from the dead. However, this weekly pattern of worship was allied to a yearly pattern which revolved around Easter."[2]

The gathering of Christians on Sunday is attested in not only the New Testament but in our earliest description of worship outside of the New Testament by Justin Martyr, wherein he says, "On the day called Sunday there is a meeting of all believers who live in the town or the country, and the memoirs of the apostles, or the writings of the prophets, are read for as long as time will permit."[3] Drobner, in his article on Easter Homilies, states the following,

> "Easter was not only the most ancient annual feast...but also Christianity's fundamental, highest, and including Pentecost, longest feast....The two most ancient and sole extant Easter homilies from the first three centuries are dated to the same period of the oldest information that has survived about an annual feast of the Christian Easter: Melito of Sardis (AD 160-170) and Pseudo-Hippolytus (between 164/166 and the end of the 2nd Century).[4]

This agreement on the early practice of Easter can be found in various literature, but speaking to the Christian perspective on this observance would be helpful. We find that Jesus died during the Jewish Passover, with specific chronology debated based on John and the Synoptics, yet the timing was not seen as mere coincidence for the early Christians. This is especially so given Paul's words about Christ as our paschal lamb, our supper being a Passover meal, and 1 Corinthians 5:7-8 taking Passover themes and applying them to spiritual matters. Yet, there were two types of paschal or easter observances at the outset.

In the Asiatic type, there is a focus on Christology, which is the doctrine of Christ. It is an Easter observance that focused on the past and the expectation of the future eschaton.[5] This 'type' of observance is usually connected to those of the Quartodeciman persuasion, seen in Melito of Sardis. Quartodeciman is a term pointing to those who observed Easter at the same time that the Jews observed Passover. This position would be the center of the Easter debate discussed below. Yet while this Christological focus is usually connected to those who observed Easter on the Passover, "we know that the Roman Easter was not different from the Asiatic feast in its content but only in its date (the origin of the Roman Easter, however, could also date back to the primitive church)."[6]

The second type dubbed the Alexandrian type, focused on the passage of the church from the shadow to the reality and thus focused a bit more on the work of Christ as it was applied to Christ's people. It focused more on the 'here and now' effects of Christ's work and the call to live in the tension of already/not yet. Rordof, however, notes that there would eventually be a synthesis of these two views by Latin writers, who based themselves primarily on the Asiatic or Christological tradition but incorporated the Alexandrian tradition. Some of the writers this synthetization is connected with are Ambrose, Jerome, and Augustine.[7] Easter would not only be a commemoration of the resurrection but would often be the time when baptisms would occur for new converts. Additionally, Easter was not seen as a one-day event but included a fast leading up to the commemoration.

As hinted above, while Easter was observed early on in the church, it was not without controversy. However, this controversy was not in regards to whether or not to observe an annual commemoration of the resurrection but when to do it. Nick Needham helpfully summarizes the controversy surrounding Easter in the Early Church,

> "Easter was the Christian equivalent of the Jewish Passover. Christ had died at the same time that the Passover lamb was sacrificed; so Christians celebrated their Savior's death at Easter, when Jews were celebrating the Passover. The churches in Asia Minor observed Easter on the precise day of Passover, the fourteenth of Nisan (in the Hebrew calendar), which was not necessarily a Sunday. But the churches of Palestine, Alexandria, and Rome always observed Easter on a Sunday, the one that fell just after the fourteenth of Nisan. This caused a serious controversy in the 2nd century, the Quartodeciman controversy, but at the Council of Nicaea in the 4th Century the custom of Palestine, Alexandria, and Rome triumphed."[8]

In essence, in all areas where Christianity resided, Easter was observed. Yet, those within Asia Minor observed Easter on the same precise day as the Jews traditionally observed their Passover. What needs to be pointed out here is that this is not a mere continuance of the Passover that many Christians insist on today. Still, Easter is being celebrated, just in accordance with the calendar of the Jews. It would be a mistake that many make to miss the distinction being made: there is a continuity and a discontinuity in Easter and Passover.

While many individuals will look to this group in Asia Minor and say they celebrated the Passover, and "Rome" overtook that practice, this is not the case. *Christendom celebrated Easter*, which at best can be understood as a Christianized version of Passover as the Asiatic tradition may have included, but was not focused on, the Exodus, the central historical event of the Passover. Instead, the focus was on Christology and Christ's work. Connections to the Exodus were made, seen in Milito of Sardis' homily, but this was not merely continuing the Old Testament Passover, which required pilgrimages to Jerusalem, sacrifices in the Temple, and so forth that were no longer possible in the post-AD 70 context.

Many portray this as a mere joining of the Gentiles with the Jews at Passover or Gentiles essentially becoming Jewish in adopting the Old Covenant. The Passover for the Jews itself was being changed because of the temple's destruction, the Sanhedrin's disbandment, and the Passover Seder's development, which would arise years later. As noted already, the contents of the festival were the same in both the Asiatic and Roman traditions, and these traditions were distinctly Christian in focusing on the messiah that the Jews did not accept. Despite what many well-meaning Christians believe, Easter was being celebrated, not merely the Passover. The argument was whether this observance of Easter should occur "when the Jews were celebrating Passover" or not. *Most Christians* elsewhere, such as in Palestine, would observe Easter on the Sunday that immediately followed the Jewish Passover. Amata summarizes the controversy as follows,

> "In the Second century, the churches of Rome and Alexandria and numerous other Eastern and Western churches were celebrating the Easter celebration of Christ's resurrection on the Sunday immediately following the full moon of spring; the churches in Asia Minor, however, the premier of which was Ephesus, celebrated Easter on the 14th day of the full moon of spring (14th of Nisan according to the Hebrew calendar). This practice drew inspiration from the Johannine tradition, according to which Jesus, who was the true Paschal Lamb, was sacrificed the same day on which the Jews were celebrating the Passover...Eusebius [the Christian church historian] mentions numerous synods in both East and West over the course of the 2nd c. that decreed that 'the mystery of the Lord's resurrection from the dead should not be on any other day than Sunday and only on that day should the Easter fasts come to an end. Eusebius also reports the testimony of Irenaeus of Lyons of a first effort to resolve the conflict between the two liturgical practices...".[9]

It is important to stress, again, that this observance of Easter was held across all of Christendom. It is noted in our earliest Christian literature outside of the New Testament (since the 2nd century, AD 100 to 200), before Constantine was born, and it was not exclusive to Rome. This last point is important because many individuals will make it out to be a 'papist Romanish' invention when this was a universal practice even in Palestine. Regarding the differences in the dating, we find both the East and the West agreeing that Sunday, the Lord's Day, was the proper time to observe Easter against the minority view that Easter should be celebrated on the Jewish Passover. Stewart-Skyes points out that,

"Numerous methods for observing Easter and calculating the date on which it had to be celebrated were already known in ancient Christianity; nonetheless, the Council of Nicaea imposed the Alexandrian calculation on all the churches of the empire: this date was similar to the practice in Rome. As part of this calculation authorities kept in mind the spring equinox; therefore, permission to celebrate Easter before this time was not granted. Some Christians, in Syria, however, whose method of calculating Easter did not take into account the equinox, were not aware of this rule. For this reason, their Easter was occasionally celebrated on a different date."[10]

While many have made much about the 'rule' regarding the Spring Equinox, saying that the Christians implemented a pagan system rather than a Jewish system, the reality is that the Equinox played a role in both the

Jewish world and the Christian world. How much of a role it played is debated, but as we observed early on, the Jewish month Nissan, when Passover would Fall, was to be in the 'spring' season. Posner, in his article on How does the Spring Equinox Relate to the Timing of Passover, states,

"While the Sanhedrin presided in Jerusalem, there was no set calendar. They would evaluate every year to determine whether it should be declared a leap year. Several factors were considered in the course of their deliberations. The primary factor, which overrode all others, was the spring equinox. If the spring equinox would fall later than the first half of Nissan, then the year was automatically declared to be a leap year. However, it wasn't enough for Passover to fall after the equinox, when it was 'officially' spring; spring like conditions needed to be evidenced...In the 4th century CE, the sage Hillel II foresaw the disbandment of the Sanhedrin, and understood that we would no longer be able to follow a Sanhedrin-based calendar. So Hillel and his rabbinical court established the perpetual calendar which is followed today."[11]

At this point, a question arises: Why was Easter being celebrated on Sunday if we are commemorating the death, burial, and resurrection of Christ in accordance with a historical date [the Passover according to the Jewish Calendar]? The answer is more straightforward than we often realize: Jesus was resurrected on a Sunday, which was seen as the first day of the New Creation. Early Christian writers viewed this time as the climax of salvation's history and anticipation of what was to come – the already/not yet. Christians gathered on the first day of the week, as seen in the New Testament (Acts 20:7; 1 Cor. 16:2; Rev. 1:10). Immediately following the New Testament literature, Sunday was known as "the Lord's Day," and every week was a recollection of the work of Christ with a 'Passover meal' in the Lord's Supper. It was significant as the dawn of the new creation (2 Cor. 5:17), sometimes called the eighth day. Jerome, the early Christian writer, would say, "Sunday is the day of the resurrection; it is the day of Christians; it is our day" (See Appendix A).

The debate between various Christians was this: Do we commemorate the historical event of Easter on the Jewish Passover because it occurred on the Passover, or do we commemorate the historical event on Sunday because it occurred on a Sunday? Both dates moved around, and this is reflected to this day, but the Passover could be on any day of the week, not having any particular significance to the Christian faith, while the Lord was resurrected on a Sunday. Both were concerned with commemorating the historical event around the time it occurred. Still, the majority of Christians found Sunday to be more significant than the moving days of the Jewish Calendar. For example, Easter falling on a Tuesday would be less sensical in light of the significance of Sunday.

Christians were attempting to find a standardization where all of Christendom could participate in Easter at the same time. In the documents of Nicaea in 325, we don't see the invention of Easter, as we have observed it was already in practice. Instead, at Nicaea, we have a document that agreed with the earlier synods (meetings) that Easter should be observed on the Sunday following the Jewish Passover. While Nicaea tried to standardize this practice so that all of Christendom could commemorate the resurrection at the same time, divergences still occurred because of different and moving calendars. This is reflected when we examine the Western Church and the Eastern Church, particularly the Orthodox Church's observance of Easter.

Before moving into our applications, we can quote the church historian Eusebius, writing in the 4th century,

"At that time, no small controversy erupted because all of the Asian dioceses thought the Savior's paschal [Easter] festival should be observed, according to ancient tradition, on the fourteenth day of the moon, on which the Jews had been commanded to sacrifice the lamb. On that day it was necessary to finish the fast, no matter what day of the week it might be. In churches throughout the rest of the world, however, it was not customary to celebrate in this way, since, according to apostolic tradition, they maintained the view that still prevails: the fast ends only on the day of our Savior's resurrection [Sunday]. Synods and conferences of elders were held on this issue, and all were of one opinion in formulating a decree for the church through letters everywhere that the mystery of the

Lord's resurrection from the dead should be celebrated on no other day than Sunday, and only on that day should we observe the end of the paschal [Easter] fast."[12]

Eusebius notes that this opinion was held by those in Palestine, with representatives in Jerusalem, Caesarea, Rome, Palamas, Gaul, Corinth, etc. This was not the mere position of Rome. The letter that was issued from the Council of Nicaea reads, in part, as follows:

"We further proclaim to you the good news of the agreement concerning the holy Easter, that this particular also has through your prayers been rightly settled; so that all our brethren in the East who formerly followed the calculation of the Jews are henceforth to celebrate the said most sacred feast of Easter at the same time with the Romans and yourself and all those who have observed Easter from the beginning."

The letter of the Emperor on Keeping the Easter, while having antisemitic rhetoric follows in the documentation,

"When the question relative to the sacred festival of Easter arose, it was universally thought that it would be convenient that all should keep the feast on one day; for what could be more beautiful and more desirable, than to see this festival, through which we receive the hope of immortality, celebrated by all with one accord, and in the same manner? It was declared to be particularly unworthy for this, the holiest of all festivals, to follow the calculation of the Jews, who has soiled their hands with the most fearful of crimes, whose minds were blinded. In rejecting their custom, we may transmit to our decedents the legitimate mode of celebrating Easter, which we have observed from the time of the Savior's passion to the present day according to the day of the week."

Unfortunately, as hinted above, this agreement was not retained due to different calculations and calendars between Alexandria and Rome. The discussion would arise again numerous times.

History is often messy, but still, we can move on and ask, what are the takeaways? Christianity, as a whole, observed Easter, and there was no debate as to whether or not it should be observed but rather when it should be observed. By all historical accounts that we have, early Christians, both Jewish and Gentile, observed Easter, an annual celebration of the resurrection, and it was dated in relation to the Passover. While many could argue that the dating is still up for debate, Christendom agreed that the observation was permissible and important as the beginning of the New Creation. Ultimately, observing the resurrection shouldn't be a point of contention if we agree that the resurrection is worth commemorating annually.

ODDS, ENDS, AND CONCLUSIONS

$\mathscr{T}$he odds and ends regarding our contemporary celebrations of Easter can be discussed in brief. As previously mentioned earlier, the incorporation of additional elements seems to be a trend in human traditions. The question is whether or not we are okay with incorporating them personally, which ultimately becomes a matter of conscience for each family to work through. When researching some of the elements of Easter, such as the Easter bunny, I found that the origins are pretty speculative. For example, most attribute the origin of the "Easter hare" to some children from Germany. The children made up a story of a bunny who laid funny colored eggs, which was brought to America in the 1700s where the tale came to include candy and chocolate. Basically, even the origin of the bunny is hardly pagan. It was more likely just a cultural tradition or game which is not a problem or sin.

Various themes of the seasons being tied into holidays is not surprising. In pagan literature, we find spring being linked to rebirth and resurrection, new life, liberation, and so forth in the same way as Passover in various literature. The reason is simple; the seasons make those connections easy. But take what we know of the Jewish perspective of the Passover and the reality that it was on Passover that Jesus became a Passover lamb for us, died, was buried, and rose again, and all of a sudden Christians have the ultimate picture of both resurrection and new life and the rebirth of the New Heavens and New Earth. The imagery was a given and many sermons play off of this reality in church history. As far as I have been able to ascertain, the introduction of the Easter Bunny and Painted Eggs came much later and, hopefully obviously, were not elements in the Christian tradition of Easter in the first several hundred years. Yet, their origin and inclusion is debated and ultimately unclear, scholars have also debated their origins and meaning.[1] With this all said we can touch on a few points:

1) Eggs and bunnies are natural symbols of new life and resurrection in global history in the spring season. Whether or not one can give the pagan exclusive rights to God's design is not really debatable – it's God's creation.

2) Paganism cannot be boiled down to x, y, or z is pagan without x, y, and z being used in a particular act of worship for a pagan deity. Paganism denotes the

worship of a pagan deity, and a rock without a deity is just a rock. As it was pointed out earlier, pagans have utilized everything, ranging from trees to water to fire, for their pagan symbols. Still, these symbols are not owned by pagans and only become pagan when there is a worship of a deity involved. Pagans cannot claim God's creation, creatures, etc as their own, but for now, it is sufficient to say if something is not being used for the worship of a pagan deity, then it is not pagan.

3)Easter does not *need* to include any cultural elements that developed slowly over time, but they aren't inherently wrong.

That the culture has slowly secularized Christian holidays shouldn't be surprising, nor should the commercialization of holidays. To see this one can look at Saint Patrick's Day and what that turned into. It is also a bad argument to state that "because the world loves it, it must be devoid of Christ," why? Because the world loves a lot of the perks of Christianity so long as you remove the Gospel and Christ. Take for example eternal life and heaven. The world loves and wants heaven, but it will go any route but the Gospel to try to get it. It should not surprise us if this happens with other aspects of the Christian life.

Nonetheless, the history around these elements is hard to confirm one way or another though it seems as if Lutherans formulated the Easter Hare, tradition links the Easter Hare to the minds of children, and Easter eggs may have originated as symbols of resurrection and new life. In early Christian tradition, eggs were often dyed red to represent the blood of Christ and the new life that his resurrection brought. But again, because of how common rabbits and eggs are, they will be used in various contexts and for various reasons. Ultimately, the origins and meanings of Easter symbols like eggs and bunnies are complex and multifaceted, and their interpretation has varied across time and cultures. While some people may see these symbols as pagan in origin, others may view them as Christian symbols of new life and resurrection. In either case, these elements are optional and don't change when, why, and what Easter was created force.

Individuals can debate those cultural elements until the cows come home; many have put forward their positions with vigor. However, Easter began and is a Christian commemoration of the Resurrection of Christ and, in its history and beginnings, has zero ties to paganism. Whether or not pagan practices became part of the Easter tradition, like painting eggs, without a pagan deity, let alone one that someone can even name with certainty, they're just painted eggs and cultural.

This is to say, it is a matter of conscience whether you want to incorporate such traditions into the holiday or not. The "new life" element in spring falls into this category. Framed in light of the new life found in the resurrection of Christ, this element makes for a pretty thematic day, and church writings certainly made this connection as well. The Resurrection signified not only the new life of the believer but the beginning of restoration of the entire earth. Why not let them coincide as spring represents "life" after winter?

Whether one wants to call the day "Easter," "Resurrection day," or "Resurrection Sunday" is a matter of conscience. I usually call it Resurrection Sunday because of the misunderstandings surrounding the term "Easter" and how muddy those waters can become. So, while Easter egg hunts, decorations, etc., are really a matter of conscience for each individual, the church should be sure to focus on the resurrection. This should always be at the forefront, and I would even postulate that those cultural elements should be left out of local church gatherings on Sunday.

CONCLUSION

As we end this exploration of the Old Testament Feasts, Christmas, and Easter, I want to take a moment to reflect on the path we've walked together. We began this journey with doubts and questions, and now, as we approach the final pages of this book, we find ourselves with a deeper understanding of these traditions, their roots, and their place in our faith. At the end of the day, where one lands at the end of this book about whether or not Christmas or Easter is acceptable is a matter of conscience, needing prayer and reflection upon scripture.

I admitted at the outset that I never intended to delve into these topics publicly. It seemed almost absurd to spend so much time defending traditions that, at first glance, appeared riddled with paganism and excess. Still, I hope this volume has revealed that these traditions are ideally not mere rituals but symbols that point us to Christ. While there are elements in these holidays that are unnecessary or twisted to the extent that we forget the "reason for the season," there is recognition by many Christians that these holidays are rich reflections on the heart of Christianity—the story of God's redemption of humanity through Jesus Christ.

This book was never solely about defending or justifying traditions. It was about seeking understanding, pursuing truth, and, in some ways, seeing that the early church wasn't just picking up paganism wherever it saw fit. In the end, celebrating Christmas and Easter is not about adhering to rigid rules, building new laws, or holding onto traditions; it is about drawing closer to God's heart and experiencing His grace's richness.

As we bring this volume to a close, I leave you with this thought: Embrace the traditions that resonate with your faith, but do so with a heart that continually seeks Christ above all else. May your celebrations be filled with unbridled joy, your reflections enriched by profound understanding, and your faith deepened by the love of Christ. Love the brethren who are convicted to abstain from these celebrations and encourage them in their love for Christ.

As we move ahead, let us do so with gratitude in the journey, a commitment to unity amid diversity, and an unyielding sense of awe at our wonderful triune God.

APPENDIX A: THE SIGNIFICANCE OF SUNDAY

*T*his appendix will discuss a growing issue in contemporary Christian circles regarding the historical position of Christians on when the resurrection occurred and when Christians should meet for worship. In recent times, there has been a challenge to this historic Christian belief, with some individuals seeking to undermine it by positing that Sunday worship is unwarranted, inaccurate, and was invented by later figures in history, such as Constantine.

In this discussion, we will very briefly defend the biblical, historical, and theological position of gathering with the saints on the first day of the week. *This should be seen as a summary of the data that demonstrates* that the first day of the week, not the Sabbath, is the pattern for Christian worship and the recognized observance of the Resurrection and Lord's Supper.

A NOTE ON THE DEATH OF CHRIST AND CALENDARS

This debate often revolves around the timing of Jesus' death concerning the day of his resurrection. Positions on this issue range from Jesus dying on a Wednesday, Thursday, or Friday. It's important to note that most individuals holding these positions still recognize that the resurrection occurred on Sunday. However, some who challenge the idea of a Sunday resurrection often rely on these differences in opinion to give weight to their case.

The discussion often focuses on how Jesus could have been in the grave for "three days and three nights," as mentioned in Matthew 12:40 if he died on Friday. Some argue that this must mean Jesus was in the grave for precisely 72 hours and then insist that Jesus' crucifixion occurred on Wednesday. Still, as far as I can tell, this interpretation is anachronistic, as it imposes modern standards of precise timekeeping on the ancient era. Nonetheless, Jesus indicated that he would be killed and rise from the dead on the third day, as mentioned in Matthew 16:21, Luke 9:22, Luke 24:7, and Acts 10:39-41. The Scriptures denote "the first day of the week" [Sunday] as the "third day since these things happened (Luke 24:1, 19-21). Regardless of whether or not we can debate a Thursday or Friday crucifixion, the New Testament's emphasis is on the "first day" in regards to the resurrection (see below).

While we aren't defending a particular position on the

crucifixion in this article, it's essential to understand that in Jewish culture, a part of a day was often counted as a whole day. Jesus used a common figure of speech to emphasize the length of time he would be in the tomb, rather than literally calculating days and nights. This figure of speech can also be found in other parts of the Bible, such as in Esther 4:16 and 1 Samuel 30:12-13. Therefore, Jesus' statement about being in the heart of the earth for three days and three nights does not necessarily require a Saturday resurrection or even a precise 72-hour period but instead emphasizes the significance of his death and burial. Yet, much confusion comes from the differences in how days were reckoned overall.

To summarize, "Friday" would begin on "Thursday" at Sundown when we use our contemporary naming of the days to understand the passion narrative. "Sunday" began at Sundown on Saturday. As confusing as it may be, this means that even if we have a "Saturday Evening Resurrection," it was "Sunday" [17th day of Nissan] according to Jewish reckonings of the week. In other words, even if the resurrection of Jesus occurred on what would be considered Saturday evening in the Gregorian calendar, it would be considered "Sunday" in the Jewish calendar, based on the evening that starts the day according to Jewish reckoning.

Simply put, "Sunday" in Jewish reckoning begins at sundown on Saturday, and therefore, even if the resurrection were to occur on Saturday evening, it would still be considered "Sunday" according to Jewish timekeeping, that is, the 'first day of the week' of the Jewish week. We'll observe that the New Testament emphasizes Sunday and that the observance of Sunday gatherings is linked to the resurrection event and the first meal of Jesus with the disciples post-resurrection.

THE BIBLICAL DATA

The Gospel accounts provide us with crucial insights into the timing of Jesus' resurrection. According to the Gospel of Matthew, after the Sabbath, which was the seventh day of the week (Matthew 28:1), Mary Magdalene and the other Mary went to the tomb early on the first day of the week (Matthew 28:1). The Gospel of Mark also confirms that the women went to the tomb "when the Sabbath was past" (Mark 16:1). It was "very early on the first day of the week" (Mark 16:2). Similarly, the Gospel of Luke affirms that the women went to the tomb "on the first day of the week, at early dawn" (Luke 24:1). These biblical accounts all point to the fact that Jesus' resurrection took place on the first day of the week - Sunday. See below (my emphasis):

- "Now *after the Sabbath,* toward the dawn of *the first day of the week*" (Matthew 28:1)
- "*When the Sabbath was past*...And very early *on the first day of the week,* when the Sun had risen, they went to the tomb" (Mark 16:1)
- "But *on the first day of the week,* at early dawn, they went to the tomb" (Luke 23:56)
- "Now *on the first day of the week*" (John 20:1)

Some, specifically those who hold to a Sabbath Resurrection theory, may argue that the references to "the first day of the week" in the Gospel accounts do not necessarily indicate the day of Jesus' resurrection but rather the day when the women visited the tomb. They may propose alternative explanations for the phrasing used in the Gospel accounts, leading to a different understanding of the timing of Jesus' resurrection. However, upon closer examination, this objection lacks a solid foundation and must be added into the text.

The consistent language of timing in the Gospels, along with the reference to the Sabbath being over, strongly suggests that the first day of the week, Sunday, was indeed the day of Jesus' resurrection. Even if we consider that the resurrection did not occur on "Sunday proper" (that is, Saturday evening by Gregorian reckoning), it occurred on the first day of the week, according to the Jewish Calendar, after the Sabbath.

Furthermore, Luke, in his gospel, records the two disciples traveling to Emmaus (24:13-35), which he says occurred on the same day as the resurrection (v. 1; 13). When arriving at the village, we find Jesus appearing, breaking bread, blessing it, and giving it to the disciples (Luke 24:30). This wording harks back to Luke 22:19, the Lord's Supper, to which Luke makes a connection to the celebration of the Supper on the day of the resurrection "on the first day of the week." While the text doesn't expand beyond that, in Luke's account of the Acts of the Apostles in 20:7, we find this notion repeated with the expressions Luke uses, "the first day of the week" with a "gathering" and "breaking bread."

Further, these will be repeated in other early Christian literature (see below) and show convergence. While this does not prove a weekly pattern of gathering on the first day of the week, the significance of "the first day of the week" becomes more evident. Additionally, the practice of meeting for communion on Sundays is linked tightly with Jesus meeting with the disciples and breaking bread with them on "the first day of the week."

- "And he took bread, and when he had given thanks, he broke it and gave it to them, saying, 'This is my body, which is given for you. Do this in remembrance of me.'" (22:19)
- "When he was at table with them, he took the bread and blessed and broke it and gave it to them." (24:30)
- "On the first day of the week, when we were gathered together to break bread." (Acts 20:7)

In John's Gospel, in 20:1 and 20:19, we see another mention of "the first day of the week." In 20:19, it is described as the evening of "that day, the first day of the week," and Jesus appears to his gathered disciples. Furthermore, in John 20:26, one week later, Jesus appears again, setting yet another precedent for a gathering on the first day of the week. This finding aligns with the understanding of "The Lord's Day" and how it came to be understood as Sunday.

The term is mentioned in Revelation 1:10, which scholars have debated to mean either 1) the eschatological "day of the Lord," 2) an annual gathering for the resurrection (Easter), or 3) the first day of the week. Early Christian literature (discussed below) shows an understanding of the phrase to indicate either 2 or 3, with many scholars seeing more warrant for position 3 (for a detailed discussion on the phrase, see Richard Bauckham's contribution "The Lord's Day" in "From Sabbath to Lord's Day," edited by Carson).

While some have argued for the position of the eschatological "day of the Lord," the context of Revelation does not support this idea, even without mentioning the specific phrase used in the Greek text. The eschatological position makes little sense as Revelation is not exclusively focused on the Day of the Lord, and it would be strange to read into the verse that it was the coming of Jesus when John had his vision.

As we have seen, the New Testament portrays Sunday, "the first day of the week," as a special day for early Christians and gives special attention to it. The gospel writers seem emphatic to share this detail, and interjecting a 'Sabbath' resurrection into the text is not only unwarranted but strange given this emphasis. Another consideration is 1 Corinthians 16:2, where the Apostle Paul instructs the Corinthians to set aside their contributions on the first day of the week, with this instruction also applying to those in Galatia (v. 1). As argued historically, there is no reason for Paul to specify "the first day of the week" and assume a gathering unless it was normative. To dismiss this in light of what has been mentioned thus far would be hasty.

Lastly, regarding the Resurrection, there is another point to consider. The Apostle Paul, in his epistles, referred to Jesus as the "first fruits" (1 Corinthians 15:20, 23), drawing from the Old Testament concept of the offering of the first fruits in Leviticus 23:10–14. This powerful imagery provides a compelling argument for a Sunday resurrection, in line with the Gospel accounts. In Leviticus 23:10–14, offering the first fruits was a significant event in the Jewish religious calendar. It was to be presented on the day after the Sabbath, specifically the day after the Passover Sabbath, which was the first day of the week. This offering was a symbol of thanksgiving and consecration, signifying the beginning of the harvest and the anticipation of God's blessing upon the rest of the harvest to come.

By referring to Jesus as the "first fruits," Paul drew a parallel between the Old Testament offering and Jesus' resurrection. Just as the offering of the first fruits occurred on the day after the Sabbath, so did Jesus' resurrection take place on the first day of the week - Sunday.

Paul's use of this imagery highlights the significance of Jesus' resurrection as the first and foremost event in God's redemptive plan, signifying the beginning of a new era and the fulfillment of the Old Testament prophecies. By calling Jesus the "first fruits," Paul affirmed that Jesus' resurrection on Sunday, the day after the Sabbath, was historically accurate and theologically significant. It fulfilled the Old Testament type of the offering of the first fruits and established Jesus as the preeminent one who conquered death and paved the way for the future resurrection of all believers.

THE HISTORICAL DATA

Historically, the early Christian Church also embraced Sunday as the day of worship and celebration of Jesus' resurrection. While many conspiracies abound regarding Constantine and "the institution of Sunday as a day of worship," the reality is that we have evidence of Sunday gatherings that predate Constantine and the Council of Nicaea. Early Christian writings, such as the "Didache," an end of the first-century Christian document (see Holmes, Apostolic Fathers), and the writings of early Christians like Ignatius of Antioch and Justin Martyr, all highlight the significance of Sunday as the "Lord's Day" and the day of worship for Christians.

Let us first turn our attention to the "Didache," also known as "The Teaching of the Twelve Apostles," which is believed to have been written in the late first or early second century, making it one of the earliest Christian writings outside of the New Testament. In chapter 14 of the Didache, it is stated: "On the Lord's own day gather together and break bread and give thanks, having first confessed your sins so that your sacrifice may be pure." Here, we simply see the reference to the Lord's Day, gathering, and breaking bread.

Similarly, the writings of Ignatius of Antioch, an early Christian and martyr who lived in the late first and early second centuries, also emphasize the significance of Sunday as the "Lord's Day." Ignatius is significant as he is understood to be discipled by Peter and to have had some association with John the Apostle and John's disciple, Polycarp. In Ignatius' letter to the Magnesians, written around AD 110, Ignatius is writing to Christians who are being pressured to observe the Sabbath. He exhorts the Christians to "no longer observe the Sabbath, but live in the observance of the Lord's Day, on which also our life sprang up again by Him and His death" (Magnesians 9.1). Here, Ignatius clearly distinguishes between the Jewish Sabbath and the Christian observance of the "Lord's Day," which he associates with the resurrection of Jesus and the new life that Christians have in Him. Ignatius' letter reflects or corroborates the early Christian practice of regarding Sunday as a day of worship and commemoration of Christ's resurrection and juxtaposes it to the Jewish Sabbath.

Furthermore, in the writings of Justin Martyr, an early Christian apologist who lived in the second century, we also find references to Sunday as the "Lord's Day" and the day of worship for Christians. In his "First Apology," written around AD 155, Justin Martyr explains the Christian worship practices and states: "And on the day called Sunday, all who live in cities or in the country gather together to one place, and the memoirs of the apostles or the writings of the prophets are read" (First Apology 67).

Justin Martyr's description of Christian worship on Sunday reflects the early Christian practice of gathering for worship on the first day of the week, which was regarded as the "Lord's Day." He also mentions the reading of the Scriptures during Sunday worship, indicating the day's significance for the study and proclamation of Christian teachings. He continues, "But Sunday is the day on which we all hold our common assembly because it is the first day on which God, having wrought a change in the darkness and matter, made the world; and Jesus Christ our savior on the same day rose from the dead. For he was crucified on the day before that of Saturn (Saturday); and on the day after that of Saturn, which is the day of the Sun, having appeared to his apostles and disciples, he taught them these things, which we have submitted to you also for your consideration."

In addition, the so-called Epistle of Barnabas, dated sometime between AD 70-135 (Michael Holmes), writes against Judaizers and frames Sunday as "the eighth day." For the author, Christians have their own legitimate weekly observance, a celebration of eschatological hope. The letter says, "You see what he means: it is not the present sabbaths that are acceptable to me, but the one that I have made; on that sabbath after I have set everything at rest, I will create the beginning of an eighth day, which is the beginning of another world. This is why we spend the eighth day in celebration, the day on which Jesus both arose from the dead and, after appearing again, ascended into heaven." (15:8-9). Here, the author connects Sunday as the "eighth day," the beginning of the new creation (in a similar fashion as Justin above), "the day on which Jesus both arose from the dead and after appearing again ascended into heaven."

Lastly, Eusebius, the early church historian, further notes in his work (HE 3.27) that there were two groups of Ebionites (heretical groups that denied the deity of Christ), one of which kept not only "the Sabbath and the rest of the discipline of the Jews" but also "The Lord's Day as a memorial of the resurrection of the Savior." The other group, apparently, did not keep the Lord's Day, but what is of significance here is that the Ebionites had in common a strict observance of the Mosaic law, and a rejection of the Apostle Paul as an apostate of the faith because of his position on the Mosaic Law and 'fraternization' with Gentiles. This is significant because while they rejected Paul and held the Law, this sect, according to Eusebius, viewed Sunday worship as legitimate because of the resurrection.

CONCLUSION

To conclude, I'll quote A.T. Lincoln's discussion on the Lord's Day in "From Sabbath to Lord's Day,"

> "The first day of the week is the only day, apart from the Sabbath, to receive explicit attention in the New Testament. It figures prominently, of course, in the Resurrection narratives of all four gospels. The terminology of 'the first day of the week' occurs in Matthew 28:1, emphatically in Mark 16:2, where the narrative had already begun with "and when the sabbath was

past" in 16:1 but then begins again with "and very early on the first day of the week." It is used also in Luke 24:1 and John 20:1 to introduce the account of the Resurrection. In addition, Luke wants to make clear that the appearances to the two on the road to Emmaus and to the eleven were on that same day. John underlines that Jesus' appearance to the gathered disciples was "on the evening of that day, the first day of the week" (20:19), and that another appearance to the disciples, with Thomas present, took place on the first day of the following week, "eight days later" (20:26)...

The New Testament evidence for the prominence of the first day in connection with Christian worship (Acts 20:7, 1 Cor. 16:2 and Rev. 1:10) is scanty but, when taken together with that of the postapostolic period, it points us clearly in one direction. Acts 20:7 with its mention of the gathering to break bread on the first day of the week, is a reference to a Sunday and not a Saturday assembly. Luke's account makes only this passing reference, but the specific mention of the first day together with the purpose of the evening meeting being to break bread suggests that this was a regular occurrence in the church at Troas, and the narrative with its talk of staying for seven days in Troas and of Paul's intention to depart the next morning reads as though Paul deliberately planned to address all believers when they assembled for their weekly meeting."

As we reflect on the significance of the resurrection

each Sunday and Easter, we are reminded of the timeless truths rooted in Scripture, history, and tradition. The summary of evidence presented in this appendix shows that the early Christians, following the example of the apostles, observed the Lord's Day as a day of worship and remembrance of Christ's resurrection. Despite challenges and misconceptions, the historical position of Christians meeting on Sundays is firmly grounded in the Word of God and the early practices of the Church.

Let us not be swayed by unfounded claims, conspiracies, or revisionist theories but rather hold fast to the faithful testimony of our forefathers in the faith. As we approach Easter Sunday, may we be renewed in our commitment to gather with fellow believers, offer our praises to the risen Savior, and partake in the Lord's Supper as a cherished tradition of our Christian heritage. May the significance of Sunday continue to inspire us to live out our faith with reverence, joy, and devotion. To Him who conquered death and rose on the first day of the week, be all honor, glory, and praise, now and forevermore. Amen.

APPENDIX B: JESUS THE COPYCAT DEITY? A CASE STUDY

The famous myth propagated by skeptics is that Jesus is a mere myth based on deities who came before him. While often these myths are attributed to liberal scholars, I believe the idea can actually be traced back to the famous work of Alexander Hislop,[1]"The Two Babylons," produced during the Reformation. Hislop's influence has been resurrected in circles of skepticism and propagated in popular media, such as the film Zeitgeist, the book known as the Da Vinci Code, and the movie Religulous. The pop media's information has further spread through various images and articles online that restate the claims.

Often, the claims center on the Egyptian Deities, Horus and Osiris, although at times, other deities such as Dionysus and Mithras are included into the mix. So what are these claims, and what are we to do with them?

To summarize the claims, it will be helpful to quote one of the sources mentioned above, Religulous,

> "Written in 1280 BC, the Book of the Dead describes a God, Horus. Horus is the son of the god Osiris, born to a virgin mother. He was baptized in a river by Anup the Baptizer, who was later beheaded. Like Jesus, Horus was tempted while alone in the desert, healed the sick, the blind, cast out demons, and walked on water. He raised Asar from the dead. 'Asar' translates to 'Lazarus.' Oh, yeah, he also had twelve disciples. Yes, Horus was crucified first, and after three days, two women announced Horus, the savior of humanity, had been resurrected."[2]

The parallels between Horus and Jesus will strike Christians who read this, and the former predates Jesus, so the question is, is it true? Not only that, but the claims go beyond this, such as another name for Horus' mother was Meri, and there was a stepfather named Seb (Joseph). Additionally, Horus was allegedly born into a cave, announced by angels, and had a star and shepherds like the birth narrative of Jesus. And so on.

PRINCIPLES TO CONSIDER

Before going into the specifics of each claim, let us pretend that the claims are valid and discuss some general principles that should be remembered in these examinations.

First, similarities or parallels in themselves should not surprise us as Christians, nor do they prove the concept of Christianity copying other ancient religions. The reality is that ancient deities having supernatural births, powers, lives, and followers is nothing remarkable or unexpected for a god. As far back as those within the Old Testament era, these constructions of other deities reflect expectations of what deity would look like and how deities could solve humanity's problems and yearnings for connection to the supernatural. In addition, we can have gods who superficially have parallels but are fundamentally different. This latter point can be exemplified when comparing Judaism, Christianity, and Islam. Superficially, they are the same, but they are foundationally and fundamentally different on ket points when we dig deeper (such as Jesus as Messiah and the Son of God).

Another principle is simple: Jesus is a historical figure, which any credible historian does not doubt.[3] This is important because these other deities' myths are indeed myths, while Jesus is rooted in history. This is a key dividing line – while these myths claimed to do these miraculous things, Jesus did so in history and with witnesses.

Finally, pagan cultures were known for blending, adopting, and assimilating other religions, while Jews (generally) were not. While it is true that Jewish Mysticism and Syncretism became significant post-AD 70, this was exceptional and typically centered around *concepts and ideas*. When looking at this with pagans, we find *gods and worship* crossing into different cultures, being absorbed, condensed, etc.

For example, Horus himself is thought to have become the god Apollo for the Greeks. This is important because it would seem more likely for pagan cults to mix and match Christian elements into their views than the other way around. These principles are crucial to navigating these topics; nonetheless, when we look into the claims regarding the Egyptian Deities of Horus and Osiris, we find the evidence of parallels severely lacking. Instead of Jesus being a copy of Horus, we find that Horus and company are bent to sound like Jesus.[4]

Here, we will examine Horus as a case study and demonstrate the issue of pick-and-pull rhetoric.

HORUS AND OSIRIS

So, who is Horus? Horus was an important deity in Egypt, depicted with a falcon head and a double crown. The Pharaohs of Egypt were associated with Horus because the Pharaoh was considered the embodiment of the god. Initially, Horus was noted to be the god of war and the sky and married to Hathor. Later, Horus would be said to be the son of Osiris and Isis. At least, that's how some summarize Horus.[5] The problem, then, is that there were several figures named Horus, and each would have their own cult and mythology, which would later be merged or absorbed by "Horus Behedet."[6] Joshua Mark states, "the name 'Horus' will usually be found to designate either the older god of the first five or the son of Isis and Osiris who defeated his uncle Set and restored order to the land."[7]

With this said, much of our interest lies in the Osiris Myth as it pertains to the birth of the younger Horus. After Osiris, the father of Horus, died, Isis sought the body of Osiris to revive him, but because he lacked his male genitalia, he was not whole and therefore could not rule. Thus, before Osiris' descent into the underworld, Isis became pregnant by transforming herself into a falcon, forming a golden phallus for Osiris, and flying around it to draw in his seed and become pregnant.[8]

From here, one could argue that Horus was conceived of a virgin. However, the distinction is evident when we consider the biblical narrative: Horus was conceived by the seed of Osiris, while within the biblical narrative, the emphasis is upon Jesus not being conceived of a male human seed (cf. Luke 1:26-38). One can easily discern the differences between the accounts. A theological and prophetic association in the Biblical account should be considered when comparing the two.

For example, Jesus' birth location and the virgin birth were predicted long before the birth itself, automatically placing him at odds with Horus in terms of being a copy-cat. Regarding this narrative, we also do not find Isis ever being called "Meri." Nor is "Seb" equal to Joseph, and in various accounts, Seb is described as Osiris' father, not Horus' stepfather. What about the claim that Horus was born in a cave with an angel, star, and shepherds or kings? We find that Horus was born in a swamp, hiding from Seb and demons, with a group of scorpions as bodyguards supplied by another deity.[9] This is quite distinct from the birth narrative of Christ!

What about the baptism of Horus by Anup the Baptizer, who was beheaded? This is hard to disprove because there are no accounts of Horus being baptized or a character named Anup the Baptizer. In other words, there is no evidence of such claims.

And more importantly, what about Horus' crucifixion and resurrection? In the accounts of Horus, there are few records of Horus dying, but certainly not by crucifixion. Instead, he is depicted as being cast into water in pieces and fished out by Isis' request.[10] Further, in most accounts, instead, he merges with the sun god and is reborn with the sun's rising each day.[11] In terms of the resurrection, Joshua Mark further states that

> "Egyptian religious beliefs would have rejected any such concept as a dead person returning to life on earth. Even Osiris, the great god and first king, was not allowed to return to his place on earth after death."[12]

While Mark believes that the *worship* of Isis influenced Christianity (particularly on iconography in relation to Mary in Alexandria), which is another debate for a different day, he states,

188

"This is not to say, however, that Christianity is simply the Isis cult re-packaged nor that Horus was the proto- type for the risen Christ."[13]

In his critique of Tom Harpur's work, The Pagan Christ, which tries to tie Horus and Jesus together, he says firmly that "his most serious offense is the claim that Horus and Jesus share 'remarkable similarities." Further,

"This claim, which is quite obviously false to anyone who knows the stories of the two figures, has become the best known of the book. Unfortunately, many readers who do not know the original stories take Harpur's claims as legitimate scholarship when they are not. To cite only a few examples, Harpur asserts that both Horus and Jesus were born in a cave - this is false, Horus was born in the Delta swamps and Jesus in a stable; both births were announced by an angel - also false, as the concept of the angel, a messenger of God, is absent from Egyptian beliefs; Horus and Jesus were both baptized - false, baptism was not practiced by Egyptians; both Horus and Jesus were tempted in the wilderness - false, Horus battled Set in many different regions, including the arid desert while the gospel stories make clear that Jesus was tempted in the desert or the wilderness; Horus and Jesus were both visited by Three Wise Men - false, Horus is never visited by wise men and, even more damaging to Harpur's 'scholar- ship', there are not 'three wise men' mentioned in the Bible which only references `wise men' who bring three kinds of gifts; Horus and Jesus both raised the dead back to life - false, Horus had nothing to do with raising Osiris or anyone else from the dead."[14]

Mapping out the data we have received on the topic of Horus, we see the following:

Claims Vs. What We Know:

- Born of a Virgin - Debatable
- Had 12 disciples - Had between 4-20 followers in different accounts
- Born in a Cave - Born in a Swamp
- Birth Announced by an Angel- No evidence
- Birth signaled by a star - No evidence
- Birth met with three kings - No evidence (Jesus was met with Magi, anyway, not kings).
- Teacher at the age of 12 and baptized - No evidence
- Tempted in a desert - Battled in various regions
- Died and raised back to life - No evidence
- Raised other dead back to life - Had nothing to do with raising anyone from the dead

When we start digging into other claims of deities that Jesus is a copycat of, we find a similar problem. Ultimately, we find the following:

1. Many parallel claims lack evidence.
2. Parallels that seem to be found are those that are generally connected to what people would expect from deities (such as performing miracles)
3. Parallels that are close often are still superficially similar rather than fundamentally similar (i.e., the virgin birth of Horus).

NOTES

INTRODUCTION

1. I'm quite confident that in this time my hair and beard turned slightly green as I considered moving to Mount Crumpit.
2. Some Protestants opposed it as well, namely Lutherans from my observations.
3. A fascinating observation is that I have not seen any documentation of pushback against these celebrations in the early church.

1. THE FEASTS

1. Larry Walker, Holman Illustrated Bible Dictionary, s.v. "FESTI-VALS," paragraph 6088.
2. Also Josephus (Ant. 14.21; 17.213; 18.29)
3. The name of the 400 years in between the Old Testament and New Testament.
4. See Part 2 - "Christmas and Paganism"

3. JEWISH IDENTITY AND KEEPING THE FEASTS

1. James D. G. Dunn, *The Epistles to the Colossians and to Philemon: A Commentary on the Greek Text*, New International Greek Testament Commentary. Accordance electronic ed. (Grand Rapids: Eerdmans, 1996), 175.
2. Ibid.
3. http://www.christianitytoday.com/ct/2017/march-web-only/jesus-didnt-eat-seder-meal.html?start=1
4. https://www.biblicalarchaeology.org/daily/people-cultures-in-the-bible/jesus-historical-jesus/was-jesus-last-supper-a-seder/
5. An article to consider: https://www.reformedworship.org/article/december-1987/should-christians-eat-seder-meal

6. https://www.patheos.com/blogs/troublerofisrael/2017/04/should-christians-eat-the-passover-seder/

4. THE SUBSTANCE IS CHRIST AND APPLICATION

1. Or "Easter"

5. INTRODUCTION

1. I also watched Lutheran Satire's "Horus Ruins Christmas" video for "research purposes," which was an entertaining video to say the least.

6. THE POSITIVE CASE

1. Or the Feast of the Nativity of Jesus
2. Commentary on Daniel of Hippolytus, 4.23.3
3. See the discussion at: https://www.roger-pearse.com/weblog/2010/01/12/the-text-tradition-of-hippolytus-commentary-on-daniel/
4. It was called, and has been called, a "Jewish" tradition but I haven't looked to see whether or not this was an actual tradition of Jewish origin.
5. Homily on the Date of Christmas, English Translations can be found in B.E. Dunlop, "Earliest Greek patristic orations on the Nativity: a study including translations," Boston College, Boston, Mass., 2004. and at Earlychurchtexts, https://www.earlychurchtexts.com/public/john_chrysostom_homily_in_diem_natalem_domini_nostri_jesu_christi.htm
6. "CHURCH FATHERS: Apostolic Constitutions, Book V." Accessed November 19, 2020. https://www.newadvent.org/fathers/07155.htm.
7. Ibid.
8. Ibid.
9. Evans, C. F. "TERTULLIAN'S REFERENCES TO SENTIUS SATURNINUS AND THE LUKAN CENSUS." The Journal of Theological Studies, vol. 24, no. 1, 1973, pp. 24–39. JSTOR, www.jstor.org/stable/23959449.

10. On Idolatry, Ante-Nicene Fathers, Vol. 3.
11. cf. An Answer to Jews, De Corona.
12. "20,000 Martyrs of Nicomedia." Accessed November 20, 2020. https://www.oca.org/saints/lives/2020/12/28/103664-20000-martyrs-of-nicomedia.
13. cf. Sermon 202
14. Of course, if we consider that the Christians overall were seen as outcasts for not participating in much of Roman society, because of its pagan influence, it is really unlikely that they would just assimilate something for the fun of it.
15. "The Chronography of 354 AD. Part 6: The Calendar of Philocalus. Inscriptiones Latinae Antiquissimae, Berlin (1893) Pp.256-278." Accessed Novembern 21, 2020. http://www.tertullian.org/fathers/chronography_of_354_06_calendar.htm.
16. Dunlop, Beth. *Earliest Greek Patristic Orations on the Nativity: A Study Including Translations.* PhD Diss., Boston College, 2004, p.2.
17. "Philip Schaff: NPNF-213. Gregory the Great (II), Ephraim Syrus, Aphrahat - Christian Classics Ethereal Library." Accessed November 21, 2020. https://www.ccel.org/ccel/schaff/npnf213.iii.v.i.html.
18. See: https://www.hebrew4Christians.com/Articles/Christmas/christmas.html and
    https://hebrew4Christians.com/Holidays/Winter_Holidays/Christmas/Date_Revisited/date_revisited.html The articles explain the Jewish calendar, when Zachariah would be serving in the temple, and how we can get an idea when Jesus would be born based off of that.
19. See footnote, 955, of The Nativity of Jesus the Messiah from the Life and Time of Jesus, accessed here https://www.ccel.org/ccel/edersheim/lifetimes.vii.vi.html#fna_vii.vi-p35.1

7. ASSERTIONS AND ANSWERS

1. "Historia Augusta • Life of Elagabalus (Part 1 of 2)." Accessed November 21, 2020. http://penelope.uchicago.edu/Thayer/E/Roman/Texts/Historia_Augusta/Elagabalus/1*.html#3.
2. Pagan assimilation of new gods, other gods, was extremely common.
3. "Roman Emperors - DIR Aurelian." Accessed November 21, 2020. http://www.roman-emperors.org/aurelian.htm.

4. Some argue this is what happened with the Celtic triquetra and the trinity, but the topic is debated.
5. Though Christians in the early church refused instruments in worship for a long time because they were too pagan!
6. Chapter 3, "The Copycat Savior?"
7. He also says Nimrod and Tammuz are the same person. How that works, I'm not sure.
8. Ralph Woodrow, "The Two Babylons," *Christian Research Journal*, 2009, https://www.equip.org/article/the-two-babylons/.
9. Ibid.

8. CHRISTMAS TREES AND LOOSE ENDS

1. Peter Gentry and Stephen Wellum, *Kingdom Through Covenant*, 2nd ed. (Wheaton, IL: Crossway, 2018), 373
2. Ibid.
3. Ibid.
4. Ibid, 375.
5. Daniel Block, *For the Glory of God: Recovering a Biblical Theology of Worship* (Grand Rapids, MI: Baker Academic, 2017), 31.
6. Ibid.
7. Ibid.
8. You can find an image from 1521 with a tree and saint Nicholas.

9. CONCLUSION

1. Philip Schaff, *History of the Christian Church*, vol. 3 (Peabody: Hendrickson Publishers, 1888), 396.
2. Ibid, 397
3. Ibid, 394.

10. INTRODUCTION

1. Such as the order of worship, time allocated for various parts of worship, setting, etc.
2. Authors Translation

3. Corban (Κοϱβαν) appears exactly once in the Greek text and it is here in Mark 7:11. In searching the LXX, I didn't find any occurrences, however, BDAG notes that it corresponds with δωϱον which is a translation of "qorban" in the Hebrew text of Leviticus 2:1; 4; 12; 13. With these texts in mind, we see the word translated as "offering" or "gift" for God. The term, then, denotes an offering that is for God and BDAG expands to say, "and closed to ordinary human use."
4. France, NIGTC: The Gospel of Mark, p. 208, 2002, Eerdmans.

11. CELEBRATION

1. Though there are instances where such worship/altar building is instructed.

12. THE INCARNATION IN THE GOSPELS

1. Author's translation
2. Alan Thompson, *Luke*, Exegetical Guide to the Greek New Testament (Nashville, TN: B&H Academic, 2016),44.
3. I. Howard Marshall, *The Gospel of Luke: A Commentary on the Greek Text*, New International Greek Testament Commentary. Accordance electronic ed. (Grand Rapids: Eerdmans, 1978), 109.
4. Ibid.
5. Ibid.
6. Author's translation
7. Stephen Wellum, *God the Son Incarnate*, Foundations of Evangelical Theology (Wheaton, IL: Crossway, 2016), 212.
8. Manlio Simonetti and Thomas C. Oden, eds. *Matthew 1–13*. vol. 1a of Ancient Christian Commentary on Scripture. ICCS/Accordance electronic ed. (Downers Grove: InterVarsity Press, 2001), 27.

13. THE INCARNATION IN THE LETTERS OF PAUL

1. Especially if you already observe the traditional resurrection celebration, "Easter."
2. Author's Translation
3. F. F. Bruce, *The Epistle to the Galatians: A Commentary on the Greek Text*, New International Greek Testament Commentary. Accordance electronic ed. (Grand Rapids: Eerdmans, 1982), 196.
4. Ibid,194.
5. One example Irenaeus's work "Against Heresies."
6. Joseph Hellerman, *Philippians*, Exegetical Guide to the Greek New Testament (Nashville, TN: B&H Academic, 2015), 108.
7. Supplemental Dynamic translation - thought for thought
8. Author's Translation
9. Joseph Hellerman, *Philippians*, Exegetical Guide to the Greek New Testament (Nashville, TN: B&H Academic, 2015), 108.
10. Hellerman and Wellum disagree on this particular point, that is, how Paul uses Morphē. I see it as a both/and.
11. Stephen Wellum, *God the Son Incarnate*, Foundations of Evangelical Theology (Wheaton, IL: Crossway, 2016), 175.
12. Joseph Hellerman, *Philippians*, Exegetical Guide to the Greek New Testament (Nashville, TN: B&H Academic, 2015), 143.
13. Gordon D. Fee, *Paul's Letter to the Philippians*, Accordance electronic., New International Commentary on the New Testament (Grand Rapids: Eerdmans, 1995), 208.
14. Joseph Hellerman, *Philippians*, Exegetical Guide to the Greek New Testament (Nashville, TN: B&H Academic, 2015), 114.
15. Stephen Wellum, *God the Son Incarnate*, Foundations of Evangelical Theology (Wheaton, IL: Crossway, 2016), 177.
16. Joseph Hellerman, *Embracing Shared Ministry* (Grand Rapids, MI: Kregel Publications, 2013), 115.
17. Ibid.
18. Ibid.
19. Moisés Silva, *Philippians*, 2nd ed., Baker Exegetical Commentary on the New Testament (Grand Rapids, MI: Baker Academic, 2005), 106.

14. CONCLUSION

1. "Spurgeon: Santa or Scrooge? And 5 Thoughts for Your Christmas Day," *The Spurgeon Centerr*, https://www.spurgeon.org/resource-library/blog-entries/spurgeon-santa-or-scrooge-and-5-thoughts-for-your-christmas-day/.
2. Ibid.
3. Ibid.
4. Gordon, Bruce. (2016) "The Grinch that Didn't Steal Christmas: A Reformation Story," The Yale ISM Review: Vol. 3: No. 1, Article 6. Available at http://ismreview.yale.edu
5. Ibid.
6. Philip Schaff, *The Apostolic Fathers with Justin Martyr and Irenaeus* (Grand Rapids: Christian Classics Ethereal Library, 2002), http://www.ccel.org/ccel/schaff/anf01.html, Against Heresies, 3.19

16. CHEAP PAGANISM

1. Like Gnosticism, Pharisees, Legalism, Religious, etc
2. See also, Siniscalco's entry, Paganism in the Encyclopedia of Ancient Christianity
3. Gane, Worship, Sacrifice, and Festivals in the Ancient Near East, from Behind the Scenes of the Old Testament.
4. The same goes for Christmas being in the Winter.
5. Ibid.
6. https://www.myjewishlearning.com/article/passover-pesach-spring/

17. LINGUISTICS AND EASTER

1. See also "The Origins of the Easter Festival," by Ronald Hutton
2. Ibid.
3. https://answersingenesis.org/holidays/easter/is-the-name-easter-of-pagan-origin/
4. Some skeptics make this claim, actually.
5. http://www.easterau.com, Found in Patterson's work.
6. https://answersingenesis.org/holidays/easter/is-the-name-easter-of-pagan-origin/

7. For this point also; https://www.tbsbibles.org/page/Acts12verse4?
   fbclid=IwAR3I-NdWg-_JOnXFQ_4bzrvW-
   qnVs6Kmts6Z6HPlAss_TVK09KkJcUNcFKE
8. Eusebius, the Church History, Translation and Commentary by Paul
   Maier. Kregal Academic, Grand Rapids, MI, 2017.

18. THE NEGATIVE CASE

1. "History of Easter," History.Com, last modified 2009, https://www.
   history.com/topics/holidays/history-of-easter.
2. Ibid.
3. Quite humorously, when sharing the meme that says Easter was
   connected to a pagan goddess, social media fact checkers flagged it
   as false, "Easter has no connection to a pagan goddess."
4. History for Atheists discusses this issue
5. https://centerforinquiry.org/blog/holy-ishtar-our-own-false-claim-
   rises-from-the-dead/
6. Ibid.

19. THE POSITIVE CASE AND THE CONTROVERSY OF EASTER

1. He holds that the dating of Christmas was influenced by pagan
   festivities, p. 158 in 2000 Years of Christ's Power vol. 1
2. Ibid, 79.
3. First Apology, 67. c. AD 100 - 165
4. Encyclopedia of Ancient Christianity, Easter Homilies, H.R. Drobner
5. See Encyclopedia of Ancient Christianity, Easter, Rordorf for more
   on this.
6. Encyclopedia of Ancient Christianity, "Easter," Rordorf
7. Ibid.
8. Nick Needham, 2000 Years of Christ's Power, vol. 1 (London: Grace
   Publications Truth, 2016), 80.
9. Encyclopedia of Ancient Christianity, the Easter Controversy, B.
   Amata
10. Encyclopedia of Ancient Christianity, Protopaschites, Stewart-Sykes
11. How does the Spring Equinox Relate to the Timing of Passover:
    About the Jewish Leap Year" by Menachem Posner.

12. Church History, 5.23.

20. ODDS, ENDS, AND CONCLUSIONS

1. Many Christians have made materials showing the doubts of alleged pagan connections between these elements and Easter such as Inspiring Philosophy on YouTube, look up, Easter is not Pagan.

APPENDIX B: JESUS THE COPYCAT DEITY? A CASE STUDY

1. To read more on Hislop's work and Methodology, see Ralph Woodrow's "The Two Babylons," Christian Research Journal, 2009, https://www.equip.org/article/the-two-babylons/
2. Religulous, Larry Charles, Santa Monica: Lionsgate, 2008.
3. Even outspoken skeptic Bart Ehrman has written on this reality and has sought to correct skeptics who claim otherwise.
4. J. Warner Wallace has a great illustration to this point in his article "Jesus is a Myth, Just like President Kennedy," See: https://cold casechristianity.com/writings/jesus-is-a-myth-just-like-president-kennedy/
5. https://egyptianmuseum.org/deities-horus
6. https://ancientegyptonline.co.uk/horus/, p. 2
7. Mark, J. J. (2016, March 16). Horus. World History Encyclopedia. Retrieved from https://www.worldhistory.org/Horus/
8. Ibid.
9. Ibid.
10. The Oxford Essential Guide to Egyptian Mythology, "Horus"
11. See Wallace's Discussion, https://coldcasechristianity.com/writings/is-jesus-simply-a-retelling-of-the-horus-myth/
12. Mark, J. J. (2016, March 16). Horus. World History Encyclopedia. Retrieved from https://www.worldhistory.org/Horus/
13. Ibid.
14. Ibid.

SELECT BIBLIOGRAPHY

__Bede. "Ecclesiastical History of the English People." Last modified 2009. https://www.britannica.com/topic/Ecclesiastical-History-of-the-English-People.

__Block, Daniel. For the Glory of God: Recovering a Biblical Theology of Worship. Grand Rapids, MI: Baker Academic, 2017.

__Bruce, F. F. The Epistle to the Galatians: A Commentary on the Greek Text. Accordance electronic. New International Greek Testament Commentary. Grand Rapids: Eerdmans, 1982.

__Butler, Trent C., Chad Brand, Charles Draper, and Archie England, eds. Holman Dictionary. Accordance electronic. Holman Illustrated Bible Dictionary. Nashville: B&H Publishing Group, 2003.

__Calivas, Alkiviadis. "The Origins of Pascha and Great Week." Last modified 1992. https://www.goarch.org/-/the-origins-of-pascha-and-great-week#_edn12.

__Fee, Gordon D. Paul's Letter to the Philippians. Accordance electronic. New International Commentary on the New Testament. Grand Rapids: Eerdmans, 1995.

__France, R. T. The Gospel of Mark: A Commentary on the Greek Text. Accordance electronic. New International Greek Testament Commentary. Grand Rapids: Eerdmans, 2002.

__Fr. Andrew Stephen Damick. "No, Christmas Is Not Pagan. Just Stop." Fr. Andrew Stephen Damick. Last modified December 5, 2018. Accessed November 16, 2020. https://blogs.ancientfaith.com/asd/2018/12/05/no-christmas-is-not-pagan-just-stop/.

__Gentry, Peter, and Stephen Wellum. Kingdom Through Covenant. 2nd ed. Wheaton, IL: Crossway, 2018.

__Gordan, Bruce. "The Grinch That Didn't Steal Christmas: A Reformation Story." The Yale ISM Review 3, no. 1, Article 6 (2016). http://ismreview.yale.edu.

__Hellerman, Joseph. Embracing Shared Ministry. Grand Rapids, MI: Kregel Publications, 2013.

———. Philippians. Exegetical Guide to the Greek New Testament. Nashville, TN: B&H Academic, 2015.

__Marshall, I. Howard. The Gospel of Luke: A Commentary on the Greek Text. Accordance electronic. New International Greek Testament Commentary. Grand Rapids: Eerdmans, 1978.

__Needham, Nick. 2000 Years of Christ's Power. Vol. 1. London: Grace Publications Truth, 2017.

__Patterson, Roger. "Is the Name 'Easter' of Pagan Origin?" Answers in Genesis. Last modified 2011. https://answersingenesis.org/holidays/easter/is-the-name-easter-of-pagan-origin/.

__Pearse, Roger. "The Text Tradition of Hippolytus 'Commentary on Daniel.'" Roger Pearse, January 12, 2010. Accessed November 19, 2020. https://www.roger-pearse.com/weblog/2010/01/12/the-text-tradition-of-hippolytus-commentary-on-daniel/.

__Sanidopoulos, John. "In Defense of the Christmas Tree," n.d. Accessed November 21, 2020. https://www.johnsanidopoulos.com/2009/12/in-defense-of-christmas-tree.html.

__Schaff, Philip. History of the Christian Church. Vol. 2. Peabody: Hendrickson Publishers, 1888.

———. The Apostolic Fathers with Justin Martyr and Irenaeus. Grand Rapids: Christian Classics Ethereal Library, 2002. http://www.ccel.org/ccel/schaff/anf01.html.

__Schaff, Philip, and Henry Wace, eds. The Seven Ecumenical Councils. Accordance electronic. Vol. XIV. 14 vols. A Select Library of the Nicene and Post-Nicene Fathers of the Christian Church, Second Series. New York: Christian Literature Publishing, 1890.

__Silva, Moisés. Philippians. 2nd ed. Baker Exegetical Commentary on the New Testament. Grand Rapids, MI: Baker Academic, 2005.

__Simonetti, Manlio, and Thomas C. Oden, eds. Matthew 1–13. ICCS/Accordance electronic. Vol. 1a. Ancient Christian Commentary on Scripture. Downers Grove: InterVarsity Press, 2001.

__Thompson, Alan. Luke. Exegetical Guide to the Greek New Testament. Nashville, TN: B&H Academic, 2016.

__Wellum, Stephen. God the Son Incarnate. Foundations of Evangelical Theology. Wheaton, IL: Crossway, 2016.

__"20,000 Martyrs of Nicomedia." Accessed November 20, 2020. https://www.oca.org/saints/lives/2020/12/28/103664-20000-martyrs-of-nicomedia.

__ "Christ in the Feast of Hanukkah - Jews for Jesus." Accessed November 19, 2020. https://jewsforjesus.org/publications/newsletter/newsletter-dec-1998/christ-in-the-feast-of-hanukkah.

__"CHURCH FATHERS: Apostolic Constitutions, Book V." Accessed November 19, 2020. https://www.newadvent.org/fathers/07155.htm.

__"Do Christmas Trees Have Pagan Roots?" Answers in Genesis. Accessed November 16, 2020. https://answersingenesis.org/holidays/christmas/do-christmas-trees-have-pagan-roots/.

__"Does Christmas Have Pagan Origins? | That Ancient Faith." Accessed November 16, 2020. https://www.thatancientfaith.uk/bookreviews/perma/1576754880/article/does-christmas-have-paganorigins.html.

__"Historia Augusta • Life of Elagabalus (Part 1 of 2)." Accessed November 21, 2020. http://penelope.uchicago.edu/Thayer/E/Roman/Texts/Historia_Augusta/Elagabalus/1*.html#3.

__"History of Easter." History.Com. Last modified 2009. https://www.history.com/topics/holidays/history-of-easter.

__"How December 25 Became Christmas." Biblical Archaeology Society, September 24, 2020. Accessed November 16, 2020. https://www.biblicalarchaeology.org/daily/people-cultures-in-the-Bible/jesus-historical-jesus/how-december-25-became-christmas/.

__"Philip Schaff: NPNF-213. Gregory the Great (II), Ephraim Syrus, Aphrahat - Christian Classics Ethereal Library." Accessed November 21, 2020. https://www.ccel.org/ccel/schaff/npnf213.iii.v.i.html.

__"Roman Emperors - DIR Aurelian." Accessed November 21, 2020. http://www.roman-emperors.org/aurelian.htm.

__"Sol - Research Database - University of Groningen." Accessed November 21, 2020. https://www.rug.nl/research/portal/publications/pub(13007598-23b4-48c5-ad15-5c8f93127122).html.

__"Spurgeon: Santa or Scrooge? And 5 Thoughts for Your Christmas Day." The Spurgeon Centerr. https://www.spurgeon.org/resource-library/blog-entries/spurgeon-santa-or-scrooge-and-5-thoughts-for-your-christmas-day/.

__"TERTULLIAN'S REFERENCES TO SENTIUS SATURNINUS AND THE LUKAN CENSUS on JSTOR." Accessed November 19, 2020. https://www.jstor.org/stable/23959449?seq=1.

__"The Chronography of 354 AD. Part 6: The Calendar of Philocalus. Inscriptiones Latinae Antiquissimae, Berlin (1893) Pp.256-278." Accessed November 21, 2020. http://www.tertullian.org/fathers/chronography_of_354_06_calendar.htm.

___"What Is Donatism? | GotQuestions.Org." Accessed November 19, 2020. https://www.gotquestions.org/donatism.html.

___"Who Was the Real Santa Claus? | That Ancient Faith." Accessed November 16, 2020. https://www.thatancientfaith.uk/book-reviews/perma/1544990820/article/who-was-the-real-santa-claus.html.

___"Why Christmas Is Not Pagan." Accessed November 16, 2020. https://www.thegoodshepherd.org.au/why-christmas-not-pagan.

___Woodrow, Ralph. "The Two Babylons." Christian Research Journal, 2009. https://www.equip.org/article/the-two-babylons/.

___"Yes, Christ Was Really Born on December 25: Here's a Defense of the Traditional Date for Christmas." Taylor Marshall. Last modified December 24, 2012. Accessed November 16, 2020. https://taylormarshall.com/2012/12/yes-christ-was-really-born-on-december.html.

www.ingramcontent.com/pod-product-compliance
Lightning Source LLC
Chambersburg PA
CBHW071158130626
46553CB00004B/1709